Artificial Intelligence Revolution

This book explores the pervasive presence of Artificial intelligence (AI) in our lives, from virtual assistants and chatbots to healthcare and gaming. It delves into how AI is transforming everyday tasks and reshaping industries, providing readers with a comprehensive understanding of its impact on modern society.

SUBHRANSHU PATI

First edition

For more information, email subhranshu.pati@hotmail.com

ISBN: (print only) **9798892336949**

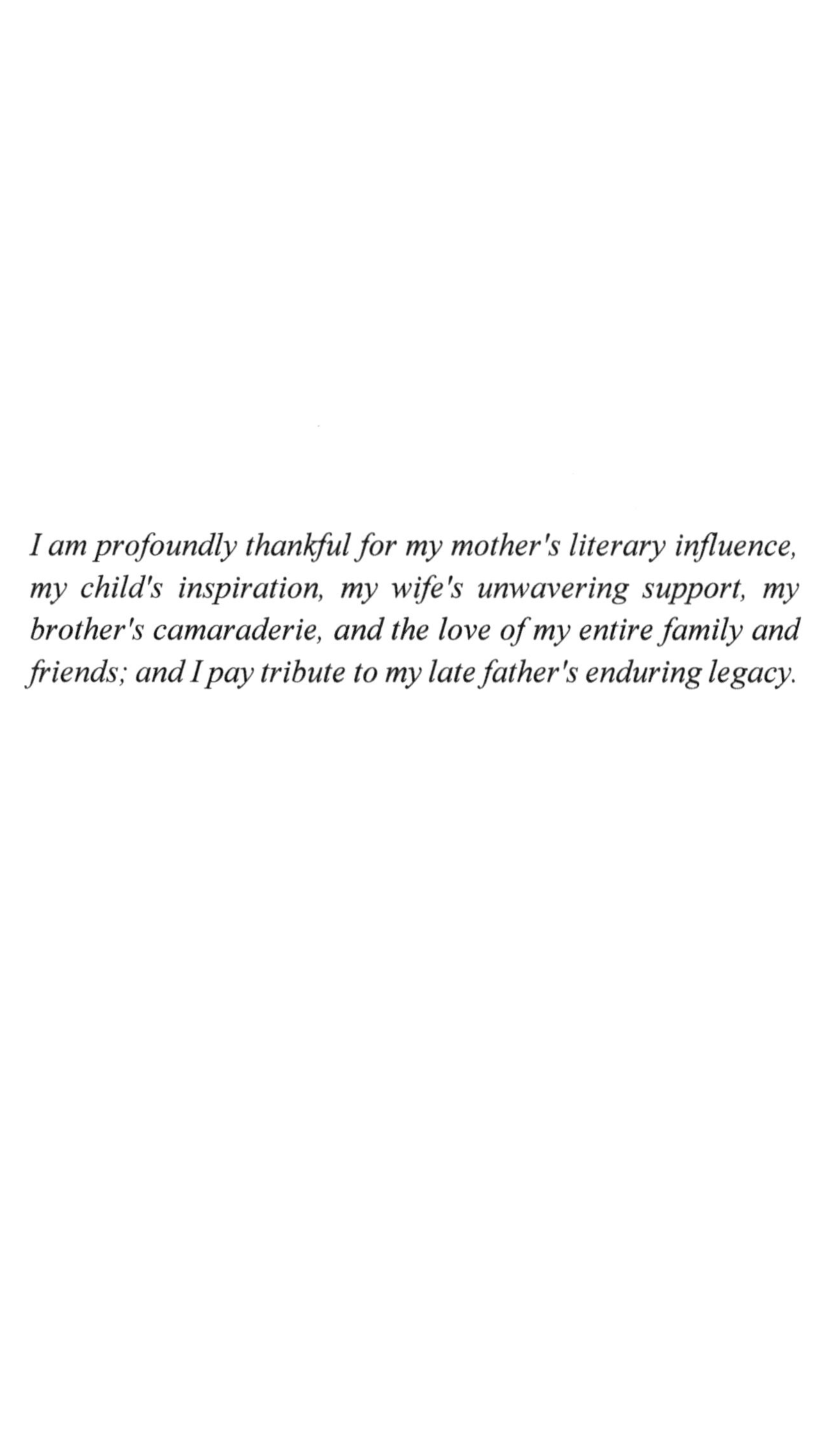

I am profoundly thankful for my mother's literary influence, my child's inspiration, my wife's unwavering support, my brother's camaraderie, and the love of my entire family and friends; and I pay tribute to my late father's enduring legacy.

Contents

Preface

In the ever-accelerating tide of technological progress, a new era has dawned - the Artificial Intelligence Revolution. As we stand on the cusp of an unprecedented transformation, this book, aptly titled Artificial Intelligence Revolution, serves as your compass in this thrilling and sometimes bewildering landscape.

Within these pages, you will embark on a captivating odyssey through the heart of artificial intelligence, exploring its myriad facets and unveiling the mysteries that have intrigued, inspired, and sometimes even intimidated us. Guided by the power of advanced technology, namely ChatGPT and Google Bard, and fuelled by extensive research into numerous AI applications and websites, this book is a culmination of passion, curiosity, and dedication.

Our exploration begins with the birth of Virtual Assistants, the digital companions that have become an integral part of our lives, simplifying tasks and enhancing productivity. We venture into the intricate world of Recommendation Systems, demystifying the algorithms that shape our preferences and influence our decisions. Fraud Detection is unravelled, showcasing how AI becomes our shield against digital threats, ensuring the safety of our online transactions and identities.

The journey takes us deeper into the realms of Image and Facial Recognition, where machines learn to perceive and understand the visual world with astonishing accuracy. Natural Language Processing (NLP) emerges as a cornerstone, enabling machines to comprehend, interpret, and respond to human language, breaking barriers and fostering global communication.

Machine Translation becomes the bridge between languages, fostering cultural understanding and global collaboration. Voice Search transforms how we interact with technology, turning spoken words into powerful commands, making our devices not just smart but intuitive. Smart Home Devices offer a glimpse into the future, where our living spaces adapt to our needs, making our lives convenient and secure.

The narrative then ventures into the intricate workings of Social Media Algorithms, exploring how our digital interactions are shaped and influenced, moulding the way we connect and engage. We explore the realm of Self-Driving Cars, where AI takes the wheel, promising a future of safer roads, reduced accidents, and efficient transportation. In the domain of Medical Diagnosis, AI becomes a trusted partner, enhancing the accuracy and speed of healthcare, potentially revolutionizing the way we approach medicine.

AI's creative process is revealed through Code Generation, where algorithms write code, pushing the boundaries of what machines can achieve. Robotic Process Automation frees human potential, automating mundane tasks and liberating creativity and innovation. Predictive Analytics becomes our crystal ball, offering insights that guide businesses and individuals alike, shaping decisions and strategies.

In the world of Customer Service, AI emerges as the friendly face behind the screen, providing assistance with unparalleled efficiency and understanding. Education undergoes a transformation, with AI becoming the personalized tutor, adapting to individual learning styles, revolutionizing the way we acquire knowledge.

This book is not merely a collection of facts and figures; it is a testament to the marvels of human ingenuity and the limitless possibilities of the digital age. It is a celebration of the researchers, developers, and innovators who have dedicated their lives to pushing the boundaries of what machines can achieve. Each chapter is a testament to the incredible progress we have made and a glimpse into the future that awaits us.

As the author, I have been both awestruck and inspired by the vast expanse of knowledge that artificial intelligence encompasses. With every chapter penned, I have marvelled at the potential of AI to transform our lives, to redefine industries, and to challenge the very notion of what it means to be intelligent.

This book is not just a documentation of technological advancements; it is an invitation. An invitation to join the revolution, to embrace the future with open arms and an inquisitive mind. It is an invitation to explore, to question, and to dream. So, dear reader, fasten your seatbelts, for you are about to embark on a journey that will not only inform and enlighten but also ignite your imagination.

Welcome to the Artificial Intelligence Revolution.

Sincerely

Subhranshu Pati

December,2023

Acknowledgments

Writing this book has been a journey of passion, perseverance, and heartfelt support. I am deeply grateful to my mother, Mrs. Sarada Pati, whose own literary prowess served as an inspiration, and whose unwavering belief in my abilities pushed me to explore my own creativity.

My sincere appreciation goes to my incredible wife, Saswati, and my precious child, Bhagyashree, for their patience, understanding, and constant encouragement. Their love has been my rock, providing the foundation upon which this book was built.

I owe a debt of gratitude to my brother and sister-in-law, Lalitanshu and Anita, for their unwavering support and belief in my vision. Their encouragement motivated me to keep going, even when the path seemed daunting.

I am profoundly thankful for the guidance and mentorship provided by Mr. Manoj Gupta, whose wisdom and belief in my writing abilities ignited the spark that led to the creation of this book. His invaluable advice has been instrumental in shaping my perspective as a writer.

This book is a realization of a childhood dream, one that I've nurtured since I can remember. The dream to create something meaningful, something that reflects my innermost thoughts and ideas. I owe my gratitude to my late father, Gayaram Pati, whose memory continues to inspire me to reach for the stars and pursue my passions fearlessly.

I extend my heartfelt thanks to my editor and publisher, whose expertise and dedication have transformed my words into a coherent and polished manuscript. Your contributions have been immeasurable and have elevated this book to its fullest potential.

To the readers, your support is the lifeblood of any writer. Your curiosity, engagement, and feedback fuel the creative process, and for that, I am profoundly thankful. Each page of this book is a testament to your belief in storytelling, and I am honoured to share this narrative with you.

To my family, friends, and teachers, your encouragement and belief in my potential have been a driving force behind this endeavour. Your unwavering support has meant the world to me.

This book is as much yours as it is mine. Thank you for being a part of this incredible journey.

Introduction

In the quiet corridors of innovation, a revolution is underway – the Artificial Intelligence Revolution. It's a phenomenon that transcends science fiction, bringing to life the dreams of generations past. In this compelling narrative, we journey through the heart of this revolution, exploring the intricate tapestry of technologies that have reshaped the world as we know it. 'Artificial Intelligence Revolution' is not just a book; it's a portal into a future where machines emulate human intelligence, revolutionizing industries, redefining relationships, and challenging the very essence of what it means to be human.

Imagine a world where virtual assistants anticipate your needs, seamlessly integrating into your daily life. Picture algorithms working tirelessly behind the scenes, curating personalized recommendations tailored to your tastes and preferences, opening doors to a universe of entertainment and discovery. Envision a future where fraud detection is not just a reactionary measure but a proactive shield, safeguarding your digital identity in an ever-connected world.

Step into the realm of image and facial recognition, where machines decode visual cues, making security robust and art more interactive. Experience the marvel of natural language processing, where machines comprehend the intricacies of human speech, enabling conversations that bridge linguistic divides and fostering connections across cultures.

Join the expedition into the uncharted territories of self-driving cars, where AI becomes the driver, ensuring safety, efficiency, and a glimpse into a future where accidents are a relic of the past. Witness the synergy between AI and healthcare, where medical diagnosis reaches unprecedented accuracy, and the treatment becomes as unique as your genetic fingerprint.

In 'Artificial Intelligence Revolution,' we uncover the secrets of code generation, where lines of logic and creativity blend, birthing software that powers our digital lives. Explore the transformation of customer service, where chatbots and virtual agents provide instantaneous, intelligent responses, redefining the standards of customer interaction.

From the intricate algorithms shaping our social media experiences to the educational tools fostering the next generation of innovators, this book navigates through diverse realms of AI applications. It delves into the promise and perils of predictive analytics, where data becomes a crystal ball, offering glimpses into the future of industries and markets.

Through captivating stories, expert insights, and thought-provoking questions, 'Artificial Intelligence Revolution' not only demystifies complex concepts but also prompts contemplation on the ethical and societal implications of our rapidly advancing technological landscape.

This book is more than a compilation of facts and figures; it's an invitation to ponder the limitless possibilities and ethical quandaries posed by the rise of artificial intelligence. So, embark on this exhilarating journey with us. Let your curiosity be your guide as we unravel the wonders, challenges, and boundless potential of the Artificial Intelligence Revolution. The future is here, and it's intelligent, inspiring, and waiting to be explored.

Who should read this book?

'Artificial Intelligence Revolution' is a comprehensive exploration crafted for a diverse audience, catering to individuals from various backgrounds, interests, and expertise levels. Whether you're a curious enthusiast, a tech-savvy professional, an aspiring innovator, or a policymaker shaping the future, this book is tailored for you.

- **Technology Enthusiasts and Curious Minds:**

If you're fascinated by the wonders of technology and eager to understand how artificial intelligence is shaping the world, this book serves as your gateway. It breaks down complex concepts into digestible narratives, allowing you to grasp the intricacies of AI without prior technical knowledge.

- **Students and Educators:**

For students aspiring to venture into the realms of computer science, engineering, or any field related to technology, this book offers invaluable insights. Educators can use this resource to inspire their students, providing real-world examples of AI applications and sparking engaging discussions in classrooms.

- **Business Leaders and Entrepreneurs:**

Entrepreneurs seeking innovative solutions for their businesses and leaders aiming to stay ahead in the competitive landscape will find practical examples and case studies illuminating the transformative power of AI. Learn how AI can optimize processes, enhance customer experiences, and drive strategic decision-making.

- **AI and Tech Professionals:**

For professionals working in the fields of artificial intelligence, machine learning, data science, or related disciplines, this book provides a holistic view of AI applications. It offers a broader perspective, enabling professionals to connect their specialized knowledge with the larger AI ecosystem.

- **Policymakers and Ethicists:**

In an age where AI technologies influence policy decisions and ethical considerations, policymakers and ethicists will find this book invaluable. It raises crucial questions about the ethical implications of AI, guiding discussions around regulations, privacy, and societal impact.

- **Science Fiction Enthusiasts:**

Fans of science fiction intrigued by the blurred lines between fiction and reality in the realm of AI will discover the actual technologies inspiring futuristic narratives. Explore how AI concepts from science fiction are becoming tangible realities, bridging the gap between imagination and innovation.

- **Anyone Seeking to Embrace the Future:**

Ultimately, this book is for anyone keen to embrace the future. Whether you're a technophile eager to adopt the latest gadgets, a parent guiding your child's educational journey, or a global citizen interested in the societal impact of technology, this book offers a roadmap to navigate the evolving landscape of artificial intelligence.

By reading 'Artificial Intelligence Revolution,' you empower yourself with knowledge, fostering a deeper understanding of the technology shaping our world. Whether you seek inspiration, information, or contemplation, this book invites you to be a part of the conversation, encouraging you to explore, question, and envision the limitless possibilities of the AI-driven future. Happy Reading!

About the Author

Subhranshu Pati is a seasoned professional in the field of Information Technology, with a strong educational background and extensive industry experience. He holds a B. Tech in Computer Science from B.C.E.T., Balasore, affiliated with Biju Patnaik University of Technology, Rourkela, Orissa.

With a career spanning 17 years, Subhranshu has dedicated his expertise to the Shipping and Logistics domain, where he has served as a Business Analyst. His comprehensive understanding of Information Technology, coupled with a keen insight into the intricacies of the industry.

This book stands as a testament to Subhranshu's passion for exploring the frontiers of Artificial Intelligence and its profound impact on shaping the future. Through his insightful writing, he invites readers to embark on a journey through the revolutionary possibilities that AI holds for our world.

You can connect with Subhranshu Pati via the following channels:

LinkedIn: www.linkedin.com/in/subhranshu-pati-functional-consultant

Facebook: https://www.facebook.com/patisubhranshu223

Twitter / X: https://x.com/SubhranshuPati

Instagram: https://instagram.com/hi.subhranshu

Email: subhranshu.pati@hotmail.com

How this book is structured?

This Book Explain, how Artificial intelligence (AI) is playing very important role now a days. AI is the ability of a machine to perform tasks that typically require human intelligence. This includes tasks such as understanding and responding to natural language, recognizing and classifying objects, and making decisions in complex environments.

AI is powered by machine learning, which is a type of computer science that allows computers to learn without being explicitly programmed. Machine learning algorithms can be trained on large amounts of data to learn patterns and make predictions.

AI is being used in a wide range of applications today. Here are top 16 AI applications that are getting used by all users in today's life.

Chapter-1: Virtual assistants: Virtual assistants like Siri, Alexa, and Google Assistant are used by millions of people around the world to perform a variety of tasks, such as setting alarms, playing music, making calls, and getting information.

Example: Using a virtual assistant to set a reminder to pick up your kids from school, or to play your favourite playlist while you're cooking dinner.

Chapter-2: Recommendation systems: Recommendation systems are used by e-commerce platforms, streaming services, and other websites to suggest products, content, and experiences that users are likely to be interested in.

Example: Using a recommendation system to find new products to buy on Amazon, or to discover new movies to watch on Netflix.

Chapter-3: Fraud detection: AI is used by financial institutions to detect fraudulent transactions and protect customers from identity theft.

Example: Using AI-powered fraud detection systems to protect your bank account from unauthorized charges.

Chapter-4: Image and facial recognition: AI is used to develop image and facial recognition systems that can identify objects and people in images and videos.

Example: Using image recognition to unlock your smartphone with your face, or to search for photos of your friends on social media.

Chapter-5: Natural language processing (NLP): NLP is a field of AI that deals with the interaction between computers and human language. NLP is used in a variety of applications, such as chatbots, translation services, and text analysis tools.

Example: Using a chatbot to get customer support from a website, or using a translation service to translate a document into another language.

Chapter-6: Machine translation: Machine translation is a type of NLP that uses AI to translate text from one language to another.

Example: Using a machine translation service to translate a foreign language website into English, or to translate a personal email into a friend's native language.

Chapter-7: Voice search: Voice search is a feature that allows users to search for information on the internet using their voice.

Example: Using voice search to find directions to a nearby restaurant, or to look up a recipe.

Chapter-8: Smart home devices: Smart home devices like thermostats, lights, and speakers use AI to learn user habits and preferences, and to automate tasks.

Example: Using a smart thermostat to adjust the temperature in your home based on your schedule, or using a smart speaker to play music when you come home from work.

Chapter-9: Social media algorithms: Social media algorithms use AI to rank and filter content in users' feeds.

Example: Seeing posts from your friends and family first on your social media feed, or seeing ads for products that you're interested in.

Chapter-10: Self-driving cars: Self-driving cars use AI to navigate roads and avoid obstacles.

Example: Using a self-driving car to get a ride to the airport, or to deliver a package to a customer.

Chapter-11: Medical diagnosis: AI is being used to develop new tools and techniques for medical diagnosis. AI systems can analyse medical images and data to identify patterns and abnormalities that may indicate disease.

Chapter-12: Code generation: Code generation systems use AI to generate code in a variety of programming languages. Code generation systems can help programmers to be more productive and to write better code.

Chapter-13: Robotic process automation: Robotic process automation (RPA) is a technology that uses AI to automate repetitive tasks. RPA systems can be used to automate tasks in a variety of industries, such as customer service, finance, and manufacturing.

Chapter-14: Predictive analytics: Predictive analytics uses AI to analyse data and make predictions about future events. Predictive analytics is used by businesses in a variety of industries to make better decisions about their products, services, and operations.

Chapter-15: Customer service: Many businesses are using AI to improve their customer service. For example, AI chatbots can be used to answer customer questions and to provide support. AI can also be used to analyse customer feedback and to identify areas where improvement is needed.

Chapter-16: Education: AI is being used to develop new educational tools and technologies. For example, AI is used to develop personalized learning programs that can adapt to the needs of each student. AI is also being used to develop systems that can provide feedback to students on their work.

1. Virtual Assistants

Virtual Assistants (VAs) are sophisticated AI applications designed to provide users with interactive, intelligent, and personalized assistance. They have become increasingly popular due to advancements in natural language processing (NLP), machine learning, and voice recognition technologies. Here's a more in-depth look at AI-powered Virtual Assistants.

How Virtual Assistants Work:

a) Natural Language Processing (NLP):

Virtual Assistants utilize NLP, a branch of AI, to understand and interpret human language. NLP algorithms allow VAs to comprehend spoken or written language, enabling users to interact with them conversationally.

b) Voice Recognition:

VAs incorporate voice recognition technology to convert spoken language into text. This technology enables hands-free interaction, allowing users to command the assistant verbally.

c) Machine Learning:

Machine learning algorithms empower VAs to learn and improve over time. They analyse vast amounts of data to recognize patterns in user requests, allowing them to provide more accurate and relevant responses with each interaction.

Common Virtual Assistant Features:

a) Task Automation:

VAs can automate various tasks, such as setting reminders, sending messages, making phone calls, and scheduling appointments. Users can delegate these routine tasks to the assistant, saving time and effort.

b) Web Browsing and Information Retrieval:

VAs can search the web for information, answer factual questions, and provide real-time updates on topics like weather, news, sports scores, and stock prices.

c) Smart Home Control:

Many VAs are integrated with smart home devices, enabling users to control lights, thermostats, security systems, and other appliances using voice commands. This integration enhances home automation and convenience.

d) Navigation and Maps:

Virtual Assistants can provide directions, traffic updates, and points of interest based on user queries. They can assist users in navigating both familiar and unfamiliar routes.

e) Language Translation:

VAs with language translation capabilities can translate phrases or sentences from one language to another, facilitating communication between speakers of different languages.

f) Entertainment and Media:

VAs can play music, podcasts, audiobooks, and videos based on user preferences. They can also recommend movies, TV shows, or songs tailored to the user's taste.

Virtual Assistant Challenges and Considerations:

a) Privacy and Security:

Virtual Assistants handle sensitive information, raising concerns about user privacy and data security. Developers need to implement robust security measures to protect user data and ensure privacy.

b) Accuracy and Context Understanding:

While VAs have improved significantly, they can still misinterpret complex queries or struggle with understanding nuanced context. Continuous improvements in NLP are addressing these challenges.

c) Integration and Compatibility:

Ensuring seamless integration with various devices, applications, and services is crucial for enhancing the user experience. Compatibility issues can hinder the assistant's functionality.

d) Ethical Considerations:

As AI becomes more integrated into our lives, there are ethical considerations regarding the impact of VAs on human interaction, social behaviour, and employment.

Virtual Assistants continue to evolve, with ongoing research and development focusing on improving their capabilities, enhancing user experience, and addressing ethical and privacy concerns.

AI virtual assistants are helping people in many ways today. Here are some examples:

- **Productivity**: Virtual assistants can help people be more productive by automating tasks such as:
    - Scheduling appointments
    - Sending emails
    - Taking notes

  - Creating and managing to-do lists
  - Setting reminders
  - Managing documents
  - Translating languages
- **Information gathering:** Virtual assistants can help people find information quickly and easily, such as:
  - Checking the weather
  - Finding news and current events
  - Looking up directions
  - Translating languages
  - Researching products and services
- **Entertainment**: Virtual assistants can help people entertain themselves by:
  - Playing music
  - Telling stories
  - Playing games
  - Reading audiobooks
  - Providing streaming content
- **Accessibility**: Virtual assistants can help people with disabilities by making it easier for them to interact with technology, such as:
  - Providing voice control for devices
  - Reading text aloud
  - Magnifying screens
  - Translating languages
- **Communication**: Virtual assistants can help people communicate with others by:

- Making and receiving phone calls
- Sending and receiving text messages
- Translating languages
- Managing social media accounts

Here are some examples of tools that AI virtual assistants can use to help people:

- **Calendars**: Virtual assistants can access your calendar to schedule appointments and events, and to remind you of upcoming events.
- **Email**: Virtual assistants can access your email to send and receive messages, and to manage your inbox.
- **Contacts**: Virtual assistants can access your contacts to make and receive phone calls, send and receive text messages, and send emails.
- **Maps and navigation**: Virtual assistants can access maps and navigation apps to help you get directions and find places.
- **Music and streaming services**: Virtual assistants can access music and streaming services to play music, podcasts, and other audio content.
- **Smart home devices**: Virtual assistants can control smart home devices such as lights, thermostats, locks, and speakers.
- **Other tools**: Virtual assistants can also access a variety of other tools and services, such as:
    - To-do list apps
    - Note-taking apps
    - Document management apps
    - Translation apps

  - Social media apps
  - Video conferencing apps
  - Shopping apps
  - Travel apps

AI virtual assistants are still under development, but they are already helping people in many ways. As they become more sophisticated, we can expect to see them play an even greater role in our lives.

Here is a list of AI apps for virtual assistants:

- Apple Siri
- Amazon Alexa
- Google Assistant
- Microsoft Cortana
- Samsung Bixby
- Huawei Celia
- Tencent XiaoWei
- Alibaba AliGenie
- Xiaomi Mi AI
- Baidu Xiaodu
- Naver Clova
- Kakao NUGU
- Yandex Alice

These AI virtual assistants are available on a variety of devices, including smartphones, smart speakers, smart TVs, and cars. They can be used to perform a variety of tasks, such as setting alarms, playing music, making calls, getting information, and controlling smart home devices.

In addition to the above, there are also a number of AI-powered virtual assistants that are designed for specific industries or applications. For example, there are AI virtual assistants for customer service, healthcare, education, and more.

AI virtual assistants are still under development, but they are already having a major impact on the way we live and work. They are becoming increasingly sophisticated and capable of performing a wider range of tasks. AI virtual assistants have the potential to make our lives easier and more efficient, and to help us in a variety of ways.

2. Recommendation systems

Recommendation systems are a vital component of many online platforms, from e-commerce websites to streaming services. These systems use artificial intelligence techniques to analyse user behaviour, preferences, and interactions to provide personalized suggestions and enhance user experience. Here's a more in-depth look at AI-powered recommendation systems.

Types of Recommendation Systems:

a) Collaborative Filtering:

- **Description:**

Collaborative filtering methods make automatic predictions about the interests of a user by collecting preferences from many users (collaborating). It assumes that if a user A has the same opinion as a user B on an issue, A is more likely to have B's opinion on a different issue.

- **Types**:

  - **User-Based:** Recommends products liked by similar users.
  - **Item-Based**: Recommends products similar to those the user has liked.

b) Content-Based Filtering:

- **Description**: Content-based filtering recommends items to users based on the description of items and a profile of the user's preferences. It suggests items similar to what the user liked in the past, based on their previous actions or explicit feedback.

- **Example**: Recommending movies based on genres, actors, or directors that the user has liked before.

c) Hybrid Models:

- **Description**: Hybrid models combine collaborative filtering, content-based filtering, and sometimes other techniques to provide more accurate and diverse recommendations. By leveraging the strengths of different methods, hybrid models often outperform individual recommendation approaches.

Techniques Used in Recommendation Systems:

a) Matrix Factorization:

- **Description**: Matrix factorization techniques decompose the user-item interaction matrix into lower-dimensional matrices. By doing this, they capture latent features that can be used to make predictions. Singular Value Decomposition (SVD) and Alternating Least Squares (ALS) are common matrix factorization met

b) Deep Learning Models:

- **Description**: Deep learning techniques, particularly neural networks, can be used for recommendation systems. Neural collaborative filtering models use embeddings to represent users and items, learning complex patterns in user-item interactions. These models can capture intricate relationships in the data.

c) Reinforcement Learning:

- **Description**: Reinforcement learning models optimize the recommendation strategy over time. They use reward-based systems, where the recommendation agent receives feedback on the quality of the suggestions and adjusts its recommendations accordingly.

Challenges and Considerations:

a) Cold Start Problem:

- **Description**: Recommending items for new users (user cold start) or new items (item cold start) is challenging because there is not enough data available to make accurate predictions. Various techniques, such as content-based recommendations or hybrid approaches, can mitigate this problem.

b) Data Sparsity:

- **Description**: User-item interaction data is often sparse, meaning users have interacted with only a small subset of items in the system. Sparsity makes it difficult to build accurate models. Techniques like matrix factorization and embedding methods are used to handle sparse data.

c) Scalability:

- **Description**: For large-scale applications, recommendation systems need to process vast amounts of data in real-time. Scalable algorithms and distributed computing frameworks are essential to handle the computational demands of recommendation systems.

d) Ethical Concerns and Bias:

- **Description**: Recommendation systems can inadvertently reinforce biases present in the training data, leading to unfair or discriminatory recommendations. Ensuring fairness and addressing biases in recommendations is an ongoing challenge in the development of recommendation systems.

e) Evaluation Metrics:

- **Description**: Choosing appropriate evaluation metrics to measure the performance of recommendation systems is crucial. Common metrics include accuracy, precision, recall, and F1 score. However, the choice of metric depends on the specific goals of the recommendation system, such as maximizing user engagement or revenue.

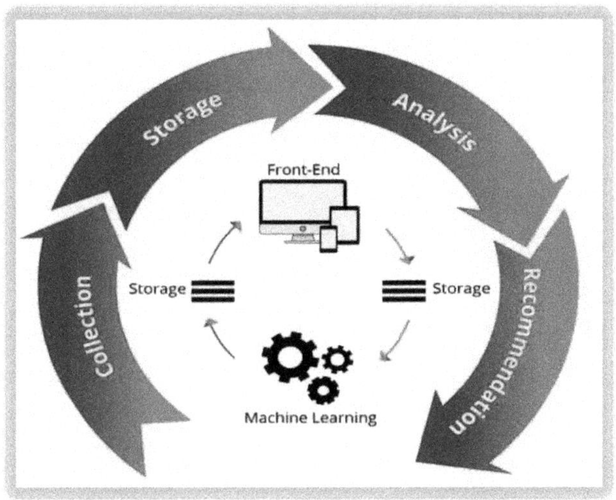

AI recommendation systems are helping in many ways today. Here are some examples:

- **E-commerce:** AI recommendation systems are used by e-commerce websites to suggest products to customers based on their past purchase history, browsing behaviour, and other factors. This helps customers to discover new products that they are likely to be interested in, and it also helps e-commerce websites to increase their sales.

- **Streaming services**: AI recommendation systems are used by streaming services such as Netflix and Spotify to suggest movies, TV shows, and music to users based on their viewing and listening history, preferences, and other factors. This helps users to find new content that they are likely to enjoy, and it also helps streaming services to retain their subscribers.
- **Social media:** AI recommendation systems are used by social media platforms such as Facebook and Instagram

to suggest friends, groups, and pages to users based on their interests and interactions with other users. This helps users to connect with people and content that they are likely to be interested in, and it also helps social media platforms to keep their users engaged.

- **News and media:** AI recommendation systems are used by news and media outlets to suggest articles and other content to readers based on their interests and reading history. This helps readers to discover new content that they are likely to find interesting and informative, and it also helps news and media outlets to increase their readership.
- **Search engines:** AI recommendation systems are used by search engines such as Google to suggest search results to users based on their previous search queries, browsing history, and other factors. This helps users to find the information that they are looking for more quickly and easily, and it also helps search engines to improve the quality of their search results.

Here are some examples of tools that AI recommendation systems can use to help people:

- **Machine learning algorithms:** Machine learning algorithms are used to train AI recommendation systems to learn patterns and make predictions. For example, a machine learning algorithm could be used to train an AI recommendation system to predict the products that a customer is likely to be interested in based on their past purchase history and browsing behaviour.

- **Big data:** AI recommendation systems use big data to learn about users' interests and preferences. For example, an AI recommendation system could use big data to learn about a user's interests and preferences based on their browsing history, social media activity, and purchase history.

- **Natural language processing (NLP)**: NLP is used to allow AI recommendation systems to understand and respond to human language. For example, an NLP algorithm could be used to allow an AI recommendation system to suggest articles to a reader based on the reader's search queries and reading history.

AI recommendation systems are still under development, but they are already having a major impact on the way we interact with the web. They are helping us to discover new products, content, and people that we are likely to be interested in, and they are making our lives easier and more efficient.

In addition to the above, AI recommendation systems are also being used in a variety of other industries and applications, such as:

- **Healthcare:** AI recommendation systems are being used to help doctors diagnose diseases and recommend treatments.
- **Education:** AI recommendation systems are being used to help teachers personalize learning for their students.

- **Finance:** AI recommendation systems are being used to help investment advisors recommend stocks and other investments to their clients.
- **Manufacturing:** AI recommendation systems are being used to help manufacturers optimize their production processes.

AI recommendation systems have the potential to revolutionize the way we interact with the world around us. They can help us to make better decisions, to discover new and interesting things, and to be more efficient and productive.

Here is a list of AI apps for Recommendation Systems:

- Amazon Personalize
- Google Recommendations AI
- Microsoft Azure Machine Learning Recommendation
- H2O.ai Driverless AI
- Recombee
- Seldon
- Oryx v2
- RecDB
- Crab
- Predictor
- LibRec
- RankSys
- LIBMF

These AI apps for Recommendation Systems can be used to build and deploy recommendation systems for a variety of industries and applications, including e-commerce, streaming services, social media, news and media, search engines, healthcare, education, finance, and manufacturing.

In addition to the above, there are also a number of AI-powered recommendation systems that are embedded in popular consumer apps, such as Spotify, Netflix, and Amazon. These embedded recommendation systems are used to suggest new music, movies, and products to users based on their listening and viewing history, purchase history, and other factors.

AI recommendation systems are still under development, but they are already having a major impact on the way we interact with the web. They are helping us to discover new products, content, and people that we are likely to be interested in, and they are making our lives easier and more efficient.

In summary, recommendation systems play a pivotal role in shaping user experiences across various online platforms. They leverage AI techniques to analyse user behaviour and preferences, providing personalized and relevant content, products, or services. The ongoing challenges in building accurate, fair, and scalable recommendation systems continue to drive research and innovation in the field of artificial intelligence.

3. Fraud Detection

Fraud detection using artificial intelligence (AI) involves employing advanced algorithms and machine learning techniques to identify and prevent fraudulent activities in various domains such as finance, e-commerce, healthcare, and telecommunications. Here's a more in-depth look at AI-powered fraud detection.

Types of Fraud Detection:

a) Traditional Rule-Based Systems:

Description: Traditional fraud detection systems use predefined rules to identify suspicious patterns in data. While effective for known fraud patterns, they might miss emerging or complex fraud schemes.

b) Machine Learning-Based Systems:

Description: Machine learning algorithms, including supervised and unsupervised learning, are trained on historical data to detect fraudulent activities. These algorithms learn patterns from data and can adapt to new and evolving fraud schemes.

Techniques Used in AI Fraud Detection:

a) Supervised Learning:

Description: Supervised learning algorithms are trained on labelled data, where historical transactions are categorized as either fraudulent or legitimate. Algorithms like decision trees, random forests, and neural networks learn to distinguish between legitimate and fraudulent patterns.

b) Unsupervised Learning:

Description: Unsupervised learning algorithms, such as clustering and anomaly detection, don't require labelled data. They detect unusual patterns in data, making them effective for identifying previously unknown fraud patterns or outliers within large datasets.

c) Deep Learning:

Description: Deep learning techniques, particularly neural networks, can analyse complex, high-dimensional data to detect intricate fraud patterns. Recurrent Neural Networks (RNNs) and Convolutional Neural Networks (CNNs) are used for sequential and structured data, respectively.

d) Ensemble Methods:

Description: Ensemble methods combine multiple machine learning models to improve accuracy and robustness. Techniques like bagging and boosting help create a more reliable fraud detection system by leveraging the strengths of different algorithms.

Data Sources for Fraud Detection:

a) Transactional Data:

Description: Transactional data, including purchase history, payment details, and user interactions, serve as the primary source for fraud detection. Machine learning models analyse these data points to identify suspicious activities.

b) Behavioural Data:

Description: Behavioural data, such as mouse movements, keystrokes, and navigation patterns, are used in fraud detection systems to create user profiles. Deviations from established patterns can indicate potential fraud attempts.

c) Device and Location Data:

Description: Information about the device used for the transaction, including device type, IP address, and geolocation, provides context for fraud detection. Anomalies, such as transactions from unfamiliar devices or locations, can trigger alerts.

Challenges and Considerations:

a) Imbalanced Data:

Description: Fraudulent transactions are often rare compared to legitimate ones, leading to imbalanced datasets. Techniques like oversampling, under sampling, and using appropriate evaluation metrics are employed to handle class imbalance.

b) Real-Time Processing:

Description: Many fraud detection systems require real-time processing to identify and prevent fraudulent transactions as they occur. This necessitates efficient algorithms and scalable infrastructures to process large volumes of data in real-time.

c) Explain ability and Interpretability:

Description: Interpretable AI models are crucial for fraud detection, especially in financial institutions, where decisions impact individuals' finances. Ensuring that AI models provide explanations for their predictions helps build trust and facilitates compliance with regulations.

d) Continuous Adaptation:

Description: Fraudsters constantly devise new tactics. Fraud detection systems need to be adaptive, continuously learning from new data to identify evolving fraud patterns effectively.

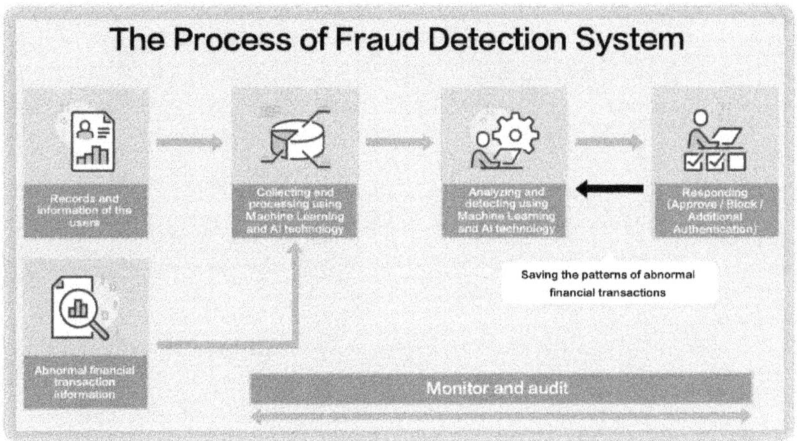

AI fraud detection is helping in a number of ways today, including:

- **Reducing fraud losses**: AI fraud detection systems can help businesses and organizations to reduce fraud losses by identifying and blocking fraudulent transactions before they are completed. This can save businesses and organizations millions of dollars each year.
- **Improving efficiency**: AI fraud detection systems can help businesses and organizations to improve the efficiency of their fraud detection processes. AI systems can automate many of the tasks involved in fraud detection, such as data analysis and pattern recognition. This can free up human resources to focus on other tasks.

- **Detecting new types of fraud**: AI fraud detection systems are able to detect new types of fraud that traditional fraud detection systems may not be able to detect. AI systems can learn and adapt over time, which allows them to identify new patterns and trends in fraud.

Here are some examples of AI fraud detection tools:

- FICO Falcon Fraud Manager: FICO Falcon Fraud Manager is a cloud-based fraud detection platform that uses machine learning to identify and block fraudulent transactions.
- LexisNexis Risk Solutions: LexisNexis Risk Solutions offers a variety of fraud detection solutions, including real-time transaction monitoring, identity verification, and fraud analytics.
- TransUnion TruValidate: TransUnion TruValidate is a cloud-based fraud detection platform that uses machine learning to identify and block fraudulent transactions.
- Experian CrossCore: Experian CrossCore is a cloud-based fraud detection platform that uses machine learning to identify and block fraudulent transactions.
- PayPal Fraud Management: PayPal Fraud Management is a cloud-based fraud detection platform that uses machine learning to identify and block fraudulent transactions.

Here are some specific examples of how AI fraud detection is being used today:

- A financial institution uses AI fraud detection to identify and block fraudulent transactions, such as credit card fraud and online banking fraud.
- An insurance company uses AI fraud detection to identify and prevent fraudulent insurance claims.

- An e-commerce company uses AI fraud detection to identify and block fraudulent orders.
- A social media platform uses AI fraud detection to identify and remove fake accounts.
- A gaming company uses AI fraud detection to identify and ban cheaters.

AI fraud detection is a powerful tool that can help businesses and organizations to reduce fraud losses, improve efficiency, and detect new types of fraud. As AI fraud detection technology continues to develop, we can expect to see even more innovative and effective ways to use AI to combat fraud.

Here is a list of AI apps for fraud detection:

- FICO Falcon Fraud Manager
- SAS Fraud Management
- Experian FraudNet
- TransUnion TruValidate
- LexisNexis Risk Solutions
- Sift
- Fraud.net
- Accertify
- ClearSale
- Kount
- Riskified
- Signifyd

These AI apps for fraud detection can be used to detect fraudulent transactions, protect customers from identity theft, and reduce fraud losses. They are used by a variety of businesses, including financial institutions, e-commerce companies, and insurance companies.

In addition to the above, there are also a number of AI-powered fraud detection solutions that are embedded in popular consumer apps, such as PayPal, Venmo, and Cash App. These embedded fraud detection solutions are used to protect users from fraudulent transactions and to reduce fraud losses.

AI fraud detection apps are still under development, but they are already having a major impact on the way that businesses and individuals protect themselves from fraud. They are helping to reduce fraud losses and to create a safer and more secure online environment.

In summary, AI-powered fraud detection systems leverage various machine learning techniques and diverse data sources to identify and prevent fraudulent activities. These systems are critical for businesses and financial institutions to protect themselves and their customers from financial losses and reputational damage caused by fraud.

4. Image and facial recognition

Image and facial recognition technologies are subsets of artificial intelligence that focus on the identification, analysis, and interpretation of visual data, particularly images and faces. These technologies are widely used in various applications, from security systems to social media platforms. Here's a more in-depth look at AI-powered image and facial recognition.

Image Recognition:

a) Object Detection:

Description: Object detection is a subset of image recognition that identifies and locates objects within an image or video. Convolutional Neural Networks (CNNs) are commonly used for object detection tasks. Applications include autonomous vehicles, surveillance systems, and image search engines.

b) Scene Recognition:

Description: Scene recognition involves categorizing images based on the scenes or environments they depict. Deep learning algorithms, especially CNNs, can learn intricate features, allowing systems to recognize complex scenes. This technology is used in robotics, environmental monitoring, and augmented reality applications.

c) Image Segmentation:

Description: Image segmentation divides an image into multiple segments or regions, enabling the understanding of object boundaries within the image. Semantic segmentation assigns a specific label to each pixel, allowing for detailed object recognition. This is essential in medical imaging, satellite imagery analysis, and industrial automation.

d) Visual Question Answering (VQA):

Description: VQA is an interdisciplinary study combining computer vision and natural language processing. It involves generating answers to questions related to images. AI models understand both image content and textual questions to provide accurate answers, finding applications in educational platforms and assistive technologies.

Facial Recognition:

a) Face Detection:

Description: Face detection identifies and locates faces within images or video frames. It's a fundamental step in facial recognition systems and is used in applications such as digital cameras, security systems, and social media tagging.

b) Face Recognition:

Description: Face recognition matches detected faces with known individuals. Deep learning models, particularly CNNs, are trained to recognize facial features and patterns. Face recognition is employed in various sectors, including security access control, law enforcement, and identity verification.

c) Emotion Recognition:

Description: Emotion recognition analyses facial expressions to identify emotions such as happiness, sadness, anger, or surprise. Machine learning algorithms can detect subtle facial cues and expressions, finding applications in market research, customer service, and mental health diagnostics.

d) Facial Landmark Detection:

Description: Facial landmark detection identifies specific points on a face, such as eyes, nose, and mouth corners. This technology is crucial for applications like augmented reality filters, facial animation in video games, and medical diagnostics.

Challenges and Considerations:

a) Privacy Concerns:

Description: Facial recognition raises significant privacy concerns. Striking a balance between security and privacy is essential, especially in public spaces and surveillance systems.

b) Bias and Fairness:

Description: AI models can be biased, leading to inaccurate results, particularly for underrepresented groups. Ensuring fairness in facial recognition systems is crucial to prevent discrimination and bias.

c) Security Vulnerabilities:

Description: Facial recognition systems are vulnerable to attacks, such as spoofing and deepfake techniques. Ensuring system robustness against such attacks is a critical challenge.

d) Regulatory and Ethical Concerns:

Description: Ethical considerations regarding the use of facial recognition technology, especially in law enforcement and surveillance, have led to increased regulatory scrutiny. Adhering to ethical guidelines and regulations is essential.

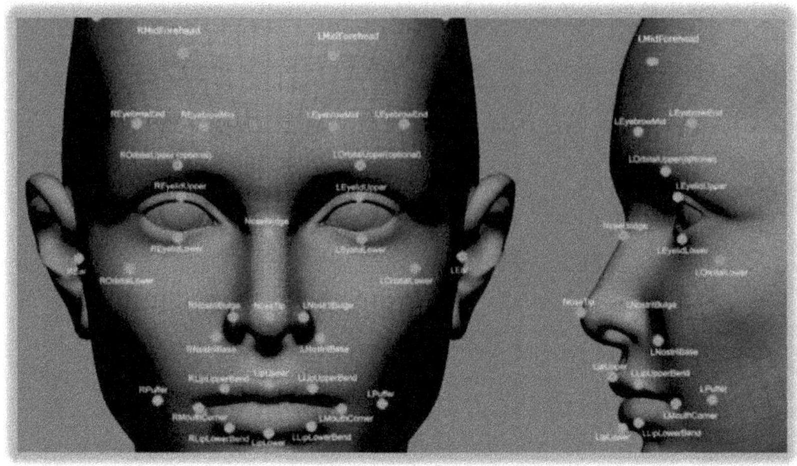

AI image and facial recognition is helping in a number of ways today, including:

- **Security**: AI image and facial recognition is being used to improve security in a variety of ways, such as at airports, borders, and other public places. AI systems can be used to identify and track people of interest, and to detect suspicious activity.
- **Convenience**: AI image and facial recognition is being used to make our lives more convenient, such as by allowing us to unlock our smartphones and other devices with our faces, and by making it easier to check in for flights and other events.
- **Accessibility**: AI image and facial recognition is being used to improve accessibility for people with disabilities. For example, AI systems can be used to help people with visual impairments to navigate their surroundings, and to help people with communication disabilities to communicate more effectively.

Here are some examples of AI image and facial recognition tools:

- **Amazon Rekognition**: Amazon Rekognition is a cloud-based image and facial recognition service that can be used to identify objects, people, and faces in images and videos.
- **Google Cloud Vision AI**: Google Cloud Vision AI is a cloud-based image recognition service that can be used to identify objects, people, and scenes in images.
- **Microsoft Azure Cognitive Services Face**: Microsoft Azure Cognitive Services Face is a cloud-based facial recognition service that can be used to identify and verify faces in images and videos.
- **IBM Watson Visual Recognition**: IBM Watson Visual Recognition is a cloud-based image recognition service that can be used to identify objects, people, and scenes in images.
- **Clarifai**: Clarifai is a cloud-based image recognition service that can be used to identify objects, people, and scenes in images.

Here are some specific examples of how AI image and facial recognition is being used today:

- Airports use AI image and facial recognition to identify passengers and to speed up the check-in process.
- Borders use AI image and facial recognition to identify people of interest and to prevent smuggling.
- Law enforcement agencies use AI image and facial recognition to identify suspects and to solve crimes.
- Social media platforms use AI image and facial recognition to tag people in photos and videos.

- Smartphone manufacturers use AI image and facial recognition to allow users to unlock their devices with their faces.

AI image and facial recognition is a powerful tool that has the potential to make our lives safer, more convenient, and more accessible. However, it is important to use this technology responsibly and ethically. AI image and facial recognition systems can be biased, and they can be used to violate people's privacy. It is important to ensure that AI image and facial recognition systems are used in a fair and transparent way, and that people's privacy is protected.

Here is a list of AI apps for image and facial recognition:

- Google Cloud Vision
- Amazon Rekognition
- Microsoft Azure Cognitive Services
- IBM Watson Visual Recognition
- Clarifai
- Cloudinary
- Kairos
- Face++
- Megvii Face++
- Yitu Technology
- SenseTime
- DeepGlint

These AI apps for image and facial recognition can be used to identify objects and people in images and videos. They are used in a variety of applications, such as:

- **Security and surveillance:** AI image and facial recognition apps are used by security and surveillance systems to identify suspects and track their movements.
- **Social media**: AI image and facial recognition apps are used by social media platforms to tag users in photos and videos, and to recommend content to users based on their interests.
- **E-commerce**: AI image and facial recognition apps are used by e-commerce companies to recommend products to customers based on their past purchases and browsing behaviour.
- **Law enforcement:** AI image and facial recognition apps are used by law enforcement agencies to identify suspects and victims, and to solve crimes.

AI image and facial recognition apps are still under development, but they are already having a major impact on the way that we live and work. They are helping to make our lives safer, more efficient, and more convenient.

In addition to the above, there are also a number of AI-powered image and facial recognition apps that are available for consumers to use on their smartphones and other devices. These apps can be used to identify objects and people in photos and videos, and to share this information with others.

AI image and facial recognition apps are a powerful tool that can be used for a variety of purposes. However, it is important to use these apps responsibly and to be aware of the potential privacy and security implications.

In summary, image and facial recognition technologies, powered by AI and deep learning, have transformative potential across numerous sectors. While they offer immense possibilities, careful attention to privacy, ethics, and fairness is crucial for their responsible and beneficial deployment in society.

5. Natural Language Processing (NLP)

Natural Language Processing (NLP) is a fascinating and complex field of artificial intelligence that focuses on the interaction between computers and human language. It enables machines to understand, interpret, generate, and respond to human language in a way that is both meaningful and contextually relevant. Here's a more in-depth look at AI-powered Natural Language Processing.

Fundamental Tasks in NLP:

a) Tokenization:

Description: Tokenization is the process of breaking down text into smaller units, such as words or sub words, known as tokens. This task is essential for various NLP applications, including language modelling and text analysis.

b) Part-of-Speech Tagging (POS):

Description: POS tagging assigns grammatical categories (such as nouns, verbs, or adjectives) to words in a sentence. It helps in understanding the syntactic structure of sentences and is a fundamental task in many NLP applications, including parsing and machine translation.

c) Named Entity Recognition (NER):

Description: NER identifies and classifies named entities (such as names of people, organizations, locations, etc.) within text documents. It is crucial for information extraction and is used in applications like news summarization and knowledge graph construction.

d) Syntax and Parsing:

Description: Syntax analysis involves parsing sentences to understand their grammatical structure. Parsing helps in identifying the relationships between words, such as subjects, objects, and predicates. Tree structures (constituency or dependency trees) are often used to represent syntactic information.

e) Sentiment Analysis:

Description: Sentiment analysis determines the sentiment or emotional tone expressed in a piece of text. It is widely used in social media monitoring, customer feedback analysis, and market research.

f) Machine Translation:

Description: Machine translation translates text from one language to another automatically. Statistical methods, rule-based approaches, and neural machine translation (using deep learning techniques) are employed in machine translation systems.

g) Question Answering:

Description: Question answering systems are designed to answer questions posed by users in natural language. These systems understand the user's query, search for relevant information, and generate concise and accurate answers.

Advanced NLP Applications:

a) Text Summarization:

Description: Text summarization techniques generate concise and coherent summaries of longer texts while preserving essential information. This is valuable for news articles, research papers, and other lengthy documents.

b) Language Generation:

Description: Language generation involves creating coherent and contextually relevant sentences or paragraphs. It is used in chatbots, virtual assistants, and content creation applications.

c) Dialogue Systems:

Description: Dialogue systems, also known as chatbots or conversational agents, engage in interactive conversations with users. These systems use NLP techniques to understand user input and generate appropriate responses.

d) Text Classification:

Description: Text classification assigns predefined categories or labels to text documents. It is commonly used in spam detection, sentiment analysis, and topic categorization.

e) Coreference Resolution:

Description: Coreference resolution identifies when two or more expressions in a text refer to the same entity. Resolving coreferences is vital for understanding the context of a document.

Challenges in NLP:

a) Ambiguity:

Description: Natural languages are inherently ambiguous, making it challenging for NLP systems to accurately interpret context, especially in tasks like machine translation and question answering.

b) Lack of Context:

Description: Understanding context is essential for accurate language processing. NLP systems struggle when faced with ambiguous pronouns, idiomatic expressions, and implied meanings.

c) Data Availability:

Description: NLP models require substantial amounts of labelled data for training. In some languages or specialized domains, obtaining large, high-quality datasets can be a challenge.

d) Ethical and Bias Concerns:

Description: NLP models can inherit biases present in training data, leading to biased predictions. Addressing these biases and ensuring fairness in NLP applications are ongoing challenges in the field.

e) Multilingual and Multimodal Challenges:

Description: Processing multiple languages and integrating text with other modalities (such as images or audio) adds complexity to NLP tasks. Cross-lingual understanding and multimodal integration are active areas of research.

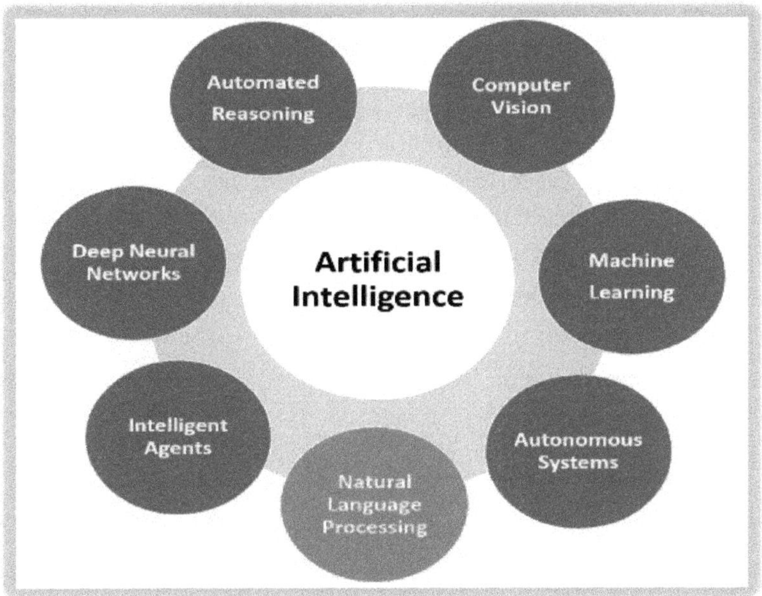

AI natural language processing (NLP) is helping in a number of ways today, including:

- Improving communication between humans and machines: AI NLP is helping to make it possible for humans to communicate with machines in a more natural and intuitive way. For example, AI NLP is used to develop chatbots that can understand and respond to human language, and to develop virtual assistants that can follow instructions and complete tasks as instructed.
- Extracting insights from text data: AI NLP is helping to extract insights from text data at scale. This is helping businesses, organizations, and researchers to better understand their customers, their products, and the world around them. For example, AI NLP is used to analyse social media data to identify trends and patterns, and to analyse customer reviews to identify areas for improvement.

- Generating creative text formats: AI NLP is being used to generate creative text formats, such as poems, code, scripts, musical pieces, email, letters, etc. This is helping writers, artists, and other professionals to be more productive and creative. For example, AI NLP is used to generate personalized email marketing campaigns and to write creative content for websites and social media.

Here are some examples of AI NLP tools:

- Google Cloud Natural Language: Google Cloud Natural Language is a cloud-based NLP platform that offers a variety of NLP services, such as text analysis, sentiment analysis, and entity extraction.
- Amazon Comprehend: Amazon Comprehend is a cloud-based NLP platform that offers a variety of NLP services, such as text classification, entity extraction, and sentiment analysis.
- Microsoft Azure Cognitive Services: Microsoft Azure Cognitive Services is a cloud-based platform that offers a variety of AI services, including NLP services such as text analysis, sentiment analysis, and machine translation.
- spaCy: spaCy is a free and open-source NLP library for Python that offers a variety of NLP features, such as tokenization, part-of-speech tagging, and named entity recognition.
- NLTK: NLTK is a free and open-source NLP toolkit for Python that offers a variety of NLP features, such as tokenization, stemming, and lemmatization.

Here are some specific examples of how AI NLP is being used today:

- A business uses AI NLP to analyse customer reviews to identify areas for improvement in its products and services.
- A social media platform uses AI NLP to detect and remove harmful content from its platform.
- A search engine uses AI NLP to better understand the intent of search queries and to return more relevant results.
- A virtual assistant uses AI NLP to understand and respond to user queries in a natural and intuitive way.
- A writer uses AI NLP to generate personalized email marketing campaigns.

AI NLP is a powerful tool that has the potential to impact many aspects of our lives. As AI NLP technology continues to develop, we can expect to see even more innovative and useful applications for this technology.

Here is a list of AI apps for natural language processing (NLP):

- Google Cloud Natural Language
- Amazon Comprehend
- Microsoft Azure Cognitive Services
- IBM Watson Natural Language Understanding
- Stanford CoreNLP
- spaCy
- Gensim
- Hugging Face Transformers

- NLTK
- MonkeyLearn
- TextBlob
- OpenAI GPT-3
- Google Bard

These AI apps for NLP can be used to perform a variety of tasks, such as:

- **Text classification**: Classifying text into different categories, such as spam or not spam, or news articles about different topics.
- **Sentiment analysis:** Identifying the sentiment of a text, such as whether it is positive, negative, or neutral.
- **Machine translation:** Translating text from one language to another.
- **Named entity recognition**: Identifying named entities in a text, such as people, places, and organizations.
- **Question answering:** Answering questions posed in natural language.
- **Text summarization:** Summarizing a long piece of text into a shorter one.
- **Text generation:** Generating text, such as news articles, poems, or code.

AI NLP apps are still under development, but they are already having a major impact on the way that we interact with computers. They are making it possible for computers to understand and respond to human language in more natural and intuitive ways.

In addition to the above, there are also a number of AI-powered NLP apps that are available for consumers to use on their smartphones and other devices. These apps can be used to perform a variety of tasks, such as translating languages, transcribing speech, and writing different kinds of creative content.

AI NLP apps have the potential to revolutionize the way that we interact with the world around us. By allowing computers to understand and respond to human language in more natural and intuitive ways, AI NLP apps can make our lives easier and more efficient.

In summary, NLP is a vibrant and continually evolving field that plays a pivotal role in many real-world applications. As advancements in deep learning and other AI technologies continue, NLP is expected to see further improvements, addressing current challenges and opening up new possibilities for human-computer interaction and understanding.

6. Machine Translation

Machine translation (MT) is a subfield of natural language processing (NLP) that focuses on using artificial intelligence to automatically translate text or speech from one language to another. Over the years, machine translation has seen significant advancements, especially with the advent of neural machine translation (NMT) techniques. Here's a deeper look into the world of machine translation.

Types of Machine Translation:

a) Rule-Based Machine Translation (RBMT):

Description: RBMT relies on linguistic rules and dictionaries to translate text. It breaks down the source text into linguistic components and rebuilds them in the target language. While accurate for specific domains and languages, RBMT systems struggle with idiomatic expressions and complex sentence structures.

b) Statistical Machine Translation (SMT):

Description: SMT uses statistical models that learn patterns from large bilingual corpora. These models generate translations based on probabilities of word sequences. While more adaptable than RBMT, SMT can still produce awkward translations, especially for languages with different sentence structures.

c) Neural Machine Translation (NMT):

Description: NMT employs deep learning techniques, particularly neural networks, to learn complex patterns and relationships in languages. It translates entire sentences or phrases at once, capturing context and nuances more effectively. NMT has significantly improved the quality of machine translations and is the dominant approach in modern machine translation systems.

Key Components of Machine Translation:

a) Encoder-Decoder Architecture:

Description: NMT models typically use an encoder-decoder architecture. The encoder processes the source sentence into a fixed-length vector representation called the context vector. The decoder then generates the target sentence based on this context vector.

b) Attention Mechanism:

Description: Attention mechanisms improve the handling of long sentences by allowing the model to focus on specific parts of the source sentence when generating each word of the target sentence. Attention mechanisms enhance the overall translation quality and fluency.

Challenges in Machine Translation:

a) Ambiguity and Context:

Description: Translating ambiguous words or phrases and understanding the context in which a word is used can be challenging. NMT models often rely on surrounding words to disambiguate meanings.

b) Rare and Out-of-Vocabulary Words:

Description: NMT models might struggle with rare or domain-specific words not present in the training data. Handling these out-of-vocabulary words is an ongoing challenge in machine translation research.

c) Language Syntax and Grammar:

Description: Different languages have varying word orders, grammar rules, and sentence structures. Translating these syntactic and grammatical differences accurately remains a challenge, especially for languages with complex grammar rules.

d) Domain Specificity:

Description: Machine translation models trained on general datasets might not perform well in highly specialized domains, such as legal or medical texts. Customizing models for specific domains is essential for accurate translations in these contexts.

Applications of Machine Translation:

a) Global Business and E-commerce:

Description: Machine translation facilitates international business by translating product descriptions, customer reviews, and communication between businesses and customers. E-commerce platforms use machine translation to expand their reach to non-native language speakers.

b) Content Localization:

Description: Media companies, including news agencies and streaming platforms, use machine translation to subtitle and dub content into multiple languages, enabling global audiences to access content in their native languages.

c) Travel and Tourism:

Description: Machine translation applications in travel include translating signs, menus, and communication between tourists and locals. Mobile apps that provide instant translation services are popular among travellers.

d) Collaborative Work:

Description: Machine translation tools are used in collaborative work environments where teams speak different languages. These tools translate conversations and documents in real time, fostering international collaboration.

e) Language Access and Inclusion:

Description: Machine translation supports language access initiatives, making information available in multiple languages for education, healthcare, and government services. It promotes inclusivity by breaking language barriers.

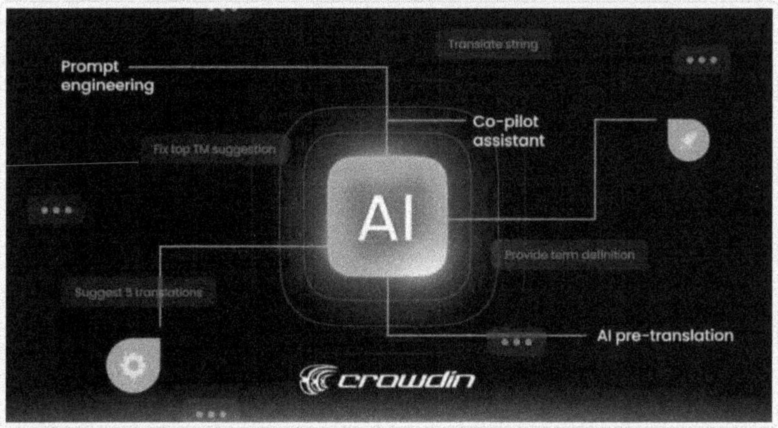

AI machine translation is helping in a number of ways today, including:

- **Breaking down language barriers**: AI machine translation is making it possible for people from different cultures and languages to communicate with each other. This is helping to break down language barriers and foster understanding and cooperation between people from all over the world.

- **Improving global communication**: AI machine translation is helping to improve global communication by making it possible for businesses, organizations, and individuals to translate their content into multiple languages. This is helping to reach a wider audience and build relationships with people from all over the world.
- **Promoting education and research**: AI machine translation is helping to promote education and research by making it possible for students and researchers to access information and resources from other countries. This is helping to advance knowledge and innovation around the world.
- **Making information more accessible**: AI machine translation is making information more accessible to people who do not speak the language in which the information is originally written. This is helping to reduce inequality and promote social justice.

Here are some examples of AI machine translation tools:

- **Google Translate**: Google Translate is a free online translation service that can translate text, documents, and websites into over 100 languages.
- **Microsoft Translator**: Microsoft Translator is a free online translation service that can translate text, documents, and websites into over 70 languages.
- **DeepL**: DeepL is a paid online translation service that offers high-quality translations for a variety of languages.
- **Reverso Translation**: Reverso Translation is a free online translation service that offers bidirectional translations for over 100 languages.

- **Bing Microsoft Translator**: Bing Microsoft Translator is a free online translation service that can translate text, documents, and websites into over 60 languages.

Here are some specific examples of how AI machine translation is being used today:

- A business uses AI machine translation to translate its website and marketing materials into multiple languages in order to reach a wider audience.
- A student uses AI machine translation to translate a foreign language textbook into their native language so that they can better understand the material.
- A researcher uses AI machine translation to translate research papers from other languages into their native language so that they can stay up-to-date on the latest developments in their field.
- A tourist uses AI machine translation to translate menus, signs, and other information into their native language while they are traveling in a foreign country.

AI machine translation is a powerful tool that has the potential to impact many aspects of our lives. As AI machine translation technology continues to develop, we can expect to see even more innovative and useful applications for this technology.

Here is a list of AI apps for machine translation:

- Google Translate
- Amazon Translate
- Microsoft Translator
- DeepL
- Reverso Translation

- Bing Microsoft Translator
- Yandex Translate
- Navcr Papago
- AI Book Translator
- ChatGPT
- Microsoft Bing
- Lingvanex Language Translator

These AI apps for machine translation can be used to translate text, documents, and even websites from one language to another. They are still under development, but they have already become essential tools for people who need to communicate across language barriers.

In addition to the above, there are also a number of AI-powered machine translation apps that are available for consumers to use on their smartphones and other devices. These apps can be used to translate text, speech, and even images in real time.

AI machine translation apps have the potential to revolutionize the way that we communicate with each other. By making it possible to translate text and speech in real time, AI machine translation apps can help us to break down language barriers and connect with people from all over the world.

Here are some examples of how AI machine translation apps are being used today:

- **Businesses**: AI machine translation apps are being used by businesses to communicate with customers and partners from all over the world. For example, a business in the United States can use an AI machine translation app to translate its website and marketing materials into Spanish to reach customers in Latin America.

- **Education**: AI machine translation apps are being used by students and teachers to learn new languages and to access educational materials from other countries. For example, a student in China can use an AI machine translation app to translate English-language textbooks and articles into Chinese.
- **Travel**: AI machine translation apps are being used by travellers to communicate with locals and to get around in new countries. For example, a traveller in Japan can use an AI machine translation app to translate signs, menus, and maps into English.

AI machine translation apps are a powerful tool that can be used for a variety of purposes. They are making it possible for people to communicate with each other across language barriers and to access information and resources from all over the world.

Machine translation continues to advance rapidly, driven by innovations in deep learning and neural network architectures. Researchers and practitioners are actively working on addressing the challenges to enhance translation quality and make machine translation systems more robust and reliable across diverse languages and contexts.

7. Voice Search

Voice search technology leverages artificial intelligence and natural language processing to enable users to search the internet, find information, and perform various tasks using voice commands. It has become increasingly prevalent with the proliferation of virtual assistants and smart devices. Here's a deeper look into the world of AI-powered voice search.

How Voice Search Works:

a) Automatic Speech Recognition (ASR):

Description: ASR technology converts spoken language into text. It uses complex algorithms and neural networks to analyse audio signals and transcribe them into words. ASR systems are trained on vast datasets to recognize various accents, dialects, and languages.

b) Natural Language Understanding (NLU):

Description: NLU processes the transcribed text to understand the user's intent and context. It analyses the structure and meaning of the words, identifying keywords and entities to comprehend the user's query accurately.

c) Query Processing and Contextual Understanding:

Description: Voice search systems consider the user's search history, location, and other contextual factors to refine search results. These systems use AI algorithms to interpret ambiguous queries and provide relevant answers based on the user's context.

Challenges in Voice Search:

a) Ambiguity and Context:

Description: Spoken language is often ambiguous, and understanding the user's intent requires considering the context. AI algorithms must decipher the meaning behind words, taking into account previous queries and user behaviour.

b) Noise and Environmental Factors:

Description: Voice search systems must work effectively in noisy environments, filtering out background noise and recognizing speech accurately. Noise cancellation algorithms and robust ASR systems are crucial for overcoming these challenges.

c) Multilingual and Accented Speech:

Description: Voice search systems need to support multiple languages and accents. Developing ASR models that can accurately transcribe diverse linguistic patterns and accents is a complex task, requiring extensive training data.

Applications of Voice Search:

a) Virtual Assistants:

Description: Virtual assistants like Siri, Alexa, Google Assistant, and Cortana utilize voice search technology. Users can ask questions, set reminders, control smart home devices, and perform various tasks using natural language voice commands.

b) Mobile Devices and Smartphones:

Description: Voice search is integrated into smartphones, allowing users to search the web, compose messages, make calls, and launch applications using voice commands. Mobile voice search has become a popular feature among users on the go.

c) Smart Home Devices:

Description: Smart home devices, including smart speakers, thermostats, and TVs, utilize voice search to provide users with hands-free control. Users can search for content, adjust settings, and perform tasks using voice commands.

d) In-Car Voice Systems:

Description: Voice search is integrated into modern cars, enabling drivers to make calls, get directions, play music, and send messages without taking their hands off the wheel. In-car voice systems prioritize safety and convenience.

e) E-commerce and Customer Service:

Description: E-commerce platforms and customer service applications use voice search to enhance user experience. Customers can inquire about products, track orders, and get personalized recommendations using voice commands.

Future Trends and Improvements:

a) Personalization:

Description: Voice search systems are becoming more personalized, understanding individual users' preferences, speech patterns, and context. Personalization enhances user experience by providing tailored responses and recommendations.

b) Multimodal Integration:

Description: Integrating voice search with other modalities, such as images and gestures, enhances user interaction. AI algorithms process diverse inputs, allowing users to search using a combination of voice, text, and visual cues.

c) Contextual Understanding:

Description: Advancements in AI algorithms enable voice search systems to understand complex queries in a more nuanced way. Systems can grasp follow-up questions, understand pronouns, and maintain context over extended conversations.

d) Privacy and Security:

Description: Ensuring user privacy and data security is a priority in voice search technology. AI models are being developed to process voice commands locally on devices, reducing the need for sending sensitive data to external servers.

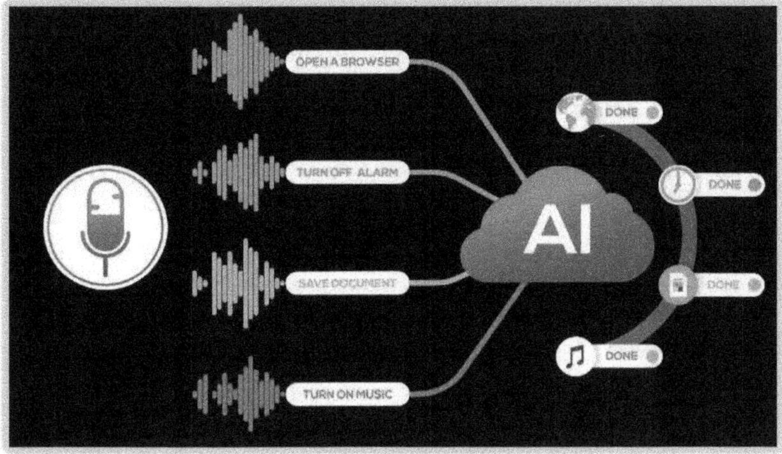

AI voice search is helping in a number of ways today, including:

- **Convenience**: AI voice search makes it easier and more convenient to search for information and perform tasks. We can simply say what we are looking for or need to do, and AI voice search will help us. This is especially helpful when our hands are full or we are in a situation where typing is difficult or impossible.
- **Accessibility**: AI voice search makes technology more accessible to people with disabilities and seniors. People who are visually impaired or have limited mobility can use AI voice search to control their devices and access information, without having to rely on others for assistance.
- **Productivity**: AI voice search can help us to be more productive by allowing us to multitask and get things done faster. For example, we can use AI voice search to control our smart home devices, send text messages, or make calls while we are doing other things.
- **Entertainment**: AI voice search can make entertainment more enjoyable and immersive. For example, we can use AI voice search to control our streaming devices, play music, or find new movies and TV shows to watch.

Here are some examples of AI voice search tools:

- **Smart speakers**: Smart speakers such as Amazon Echo and Google Nest Hub allow us to control our smart home devices, search for information, and get help with tasks using our voice.
- **Virtual assistants**: Virtual assistants such as Siri and Google Assistant are built into our smartphones and other devices, and allow us to perform tasks and get information using our voice.
- **Wearable devices**: Wearable devices such as smartwatches and earbuds allow us to use AI voice search on the go.

Here are some specific examples of how AI voice search is being used today:

- A busy mom uses her smart speaker to control her smart home devices and play music while she is cooking dinner.
- A person with a visual impairment uses their virtual assistant to navigate their surroundings and access information.
- A student uses their smartwatch to control their music and get help with their homework while they are walking to school.
- A traveller uses their earbuds to get directions and translate languages while they are on vacation.

AI voice search has the potential to revolutionize the way that we interact with technology. By making it easier and more convenient to search for information, perform tasks, and control our devices, AI voice search can improve our quality of life.

In addition to the above, AI voice search is also being used in a number of innovative ways, such as:

- **In healthcare**, AI voice search is being used to develop new diagnostic tools and to improve communication between patients and healthcare providers.
- **In education**, AI voice search is being used to develop new learning tools and to make educational content more accessible to students with disabilities.
- **In customer service**, AI voice search is being used to develop new ways for customers to interact with businesses. For example, customers can use AI voice search to get help with their orders, to make returns, and to resolve customer service issues.

AI voice search is a powerful tool that has the potential to impact many aspects of our lives. As AI voice search technology continues to develop, we can expect to see even more innovative and useful applications for this technology.

Here is a list of AI apps for voice search:

- Google Assistant
- Apple Siri
- Amazon Alexa
- Microsoft Cortana
- Samsung Bixby
- Huawei Celia
- Tencent XiaoWei
- Alibaba AliGenie
- Xiaomi Mi AI
- Baidu Xiaodu
- Naver Clova
- Kakao NUGU
- Yandex Alice

These AI apps for voice search can be used to perform a variety of tasks, such as:

- Searching the web for information
- Making calls
- Sending text messages

- Setting alarms
- Playing music
- Controlling smart home devices

Voice search apps are still under development, but they are already having a major impact on the way that we interact with technology. They are making it possible to control devices and access information in a more natural and intuitive way.

In addition to the above, there are also a number of AI-powered voice search apps that are available for consumers to use on their smartphones and other devices. These apps can be used to perform a variety of tasks, such as searching the web, transcribing speech, and translating languages.

AI voice search apps have the potential to revolutionize the way that we interact with the world around us. By making it possible to control devices and access information using our voice, AI voice search apps can make our lives easier and more efficient.

Here are some examples of how AI voice search apps are being used today:

- **People with disabilities**: AI voice search apps are being used by people with disabilities to access technology and information that they would not otherwise be able to use. For example, a person who is blind can use an AI voice search app to search the web for information or to control their smart home devices.
- **Businesses**: AI voice search apps are being used by businesses to improve customer service and to increase sales. For example, a business can use an AI voice search app to allow customers to search for products and services online using their voice.

- **Education**: AI voice search apps are being used by students and teachers to learn new concepts and to access educational materials. For example, a student can use an AI voice search app to ask questions about a topic that they are learning in school or to get help with a homework assignment.

AI voice search apps are a powerful tool that can be used for a variety of purposes. They are making it possible for people to interact with technology and access information in a more natural and intuitive way.

Voice search technology continues to evolve, driven by advancements in AI and deep learning. As these systems become more sophisticated, they are expected to provide even more accurate, personalized, and contextually relevant responses, transforming the way people interact with technology.

8. Smart Home Devices

Smart home devices, also known as home automation devices, utilize artificial intelligence and Internet of Things (IoT) technology to enhance the functionality, convenience, and energy efficiency of homes. These devices are designed to automate and control various household tasks and functions, providing users with a seamless and connected living experience. Here's a deeper look into the AI-powered world of smart home devices.

Types of Smart Home Devices:

a) Smart Assistants:

Description: Smart assistants like Amazon Alexa, Google Assistant, and Apple Siri use natural language processing (NLP) and AI algorithms to understand voice commands. They control various smart devices, answer questions, provide weather updates, and even initiate conversations with users.

b) Smart Lighting:

Description: Smart light bulbs and lighting systems can be controlled remotely through smartphone apps or voice commands. AI algorithms enable features like adjusting brightness, changing colours, and setting schedules for energy efficiency.

c) Smart Thermostats:

Description: Smart thermostats, such as Nest and ecobee, use AI to learn user habits and preferences. They automatically adjust heating and cooling settings to optimize comfort and energy usage, leading to cost savings.

d) Smart Security Systems:

Description: AI-powered security cameras and systems use computer vision to recognize people, animals, and objects. They can send real-time alerts to homeowners, analyse footage for suspicious activities, and even differentiate between familiar and unfamiliar faces.

e) Smart Door Locks:

Description: Smart locks utilize AI algorithms for features like facial recognition, fingerprint recognition, or voice recognition, enhancing security and convenience. Homeowners can remotely grant access to guests and receive notifications when doors are unlocked.

f) Smart Appliances:

Description: AI-enabled smart appliances, such as refrigerators, washing machines, and ovens, optimize energy usage, suggest recipes based on available ingredients, and provide maintenance notifications. They learn user habits to enhance efficiency.

How AI Enhances Smart Home Devices:

a) Context Awareness:

Description: Smart home devices with AI can analyse user behaviour, routines, and preferences to anticipate needs. For instance, they can adjust room temperature or lighting based on historical usage patterns.

b) Predictive Maintenance:

Description: AI algorithms monitor the performance of smart appliances and devices. They can detect anomalies and predict when maintenance is required, reducing downtime and prolonging the lifespan of devices.

c) Energy Efficiency:

Description: AI-powered smart home devices optimize energy consumption by analysing usage patterns and adjusting settings accordingly. They can turn off devices when not in use, manage power usage during peak hours, and recommend energy-saving practices.

d) Personalization:

Description: AI enables personalized experiences. Smart home devices can learn individual preferences for lighting, temperature, music, and more. They provide tailored suggestions and automate settings based on individual user profiles.

Challenges and Considerations:

a) Privacy and Security:

Description: Smart home devices collect and process sensitive data. Ensuring robust security measures, such as encryption and authentication, is vital to protect user privacy and prevent unauthorized access.

b) Interoperability:

Description: Many smart home devices come from different manufacturers, leading to interoperability challenges. Standards like Zigbee and Z-Wave aim to create a unified ecosystem, but ensuring compatibility remains a concern.

c) User Experience and Education:

Description: For widespread adoption, smart home devices need to be user-friendly. Manufacturers must invest in intuitive interfaces and user education to help users make the most of AI-powered features.

d) Ethical Considerations:

Description: Ethical concerns around AI in smart homes include issues like data collection consent, bias in algorithms, and ensuring that AI-powered devices are used responsibly and do not infringe on users' rights.

Future Trends in Smart Home Devices:

a) Integration of AI with IoT:

Description: AI and IoT technologies will become more tightly integrated. Devices will share and analyse data in real time, allowing for more intelligent automation and personalized user experiences.

b) Edge AI:

Description: Edge AI, where AI algorithms run locally on devices rather than in the cloud, will become more prevalent. This reduces latency, enhances privacy, and enables real-time decision-making in smart home applications.

c) Health and Wellness Monitoring:

Description: Smart home devices will increasingly focus on health and wellness monitoring. AI-powered sensors can analyze sleep patterns, monitor vital signs, and provide health-related recommendations.

d) Enhanced Human-Computer Interaction:

Description: Natural language processing and computer vision will improve, enabling more seamless human-computer interaction. Conversations with smart home devices will become more natural, and gesture recognition will enhance user control.

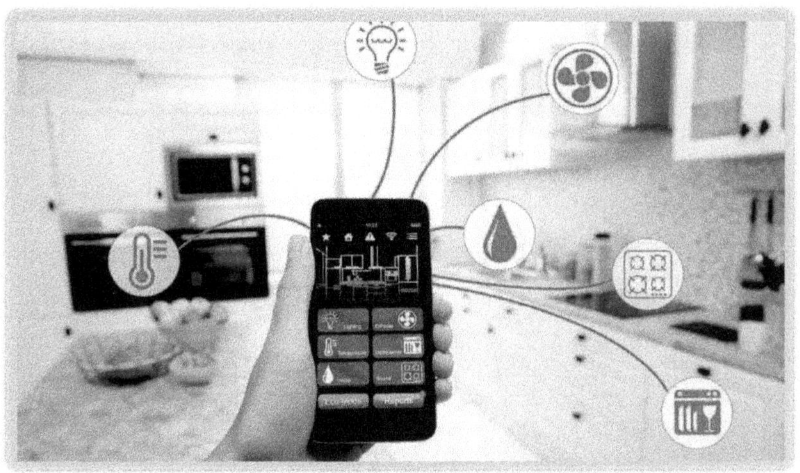

AI smart home devices are helping in a number of ways today, including:

- **Convenience**: AI smart home devices can make our lives more convenient by automating tasks such as turning on and off lights, adjusting the thermostat, and locking and unlocking doors. This can free up our time to do other things.
- **Efficiency**: AI smart home devices can help us to save energy and money by optimizing our energy consumption. For example, an AI smart thermostat can learn our daily routines and adjust the temperature accordingly.
- **Safety and security**: AI smart home devices can help to make our homes safer and more secure by monitoring for potential threats such as break-ins and fires. For example,

an AI security camera can detect motion and send us an alert if it detects something suspicious.

- **Accessibility**: AI smart home devices can help to make homes more accessible for people with disabilities and seniors. For example, a voice assistant can be used to control smart home devices without having to move around.

Here are some examples of AI smart home devices:

- **Smart speakers**: Smart speakers such as Amazon Echo and Google Nest Hub can be used to control other smart home devices, play music, set alarms, and answer questions.
- **Smart thermostats**: Smart thermostats such as Nest and ecobee can learn our daily routines and adjust the temperature accordingly to save energy.
- **Smart lights**: Smart lights such as Philips Hue and LIFX can be controlled remotely, scheduled to turn on and off at specific times, and even synced with music and movies.
- **Smart locks**: Smart locks such as Schlage and August can be locked and unlocked remotely, and even programmed to unlock automatically when we arrive home.
- **Security cameras**: Smart security cameras such as Arlo and Ring can detect motion and send us alerts if they detect something suspicious.

Here are some specific examples of how AI smart home devices are being used today:

- A family with young children uses a smart speaker to control their smart lights and thermostat. They can tell the speaker to turn on the lights when they come home from work, or to adjust the thermostat when they go to bed.

- A senior citizen uses a smart lock to allow her caregivers to enter her home without having to give them a key. She also uses a smart security camera to monitor her home when she is away.
- A person with a disability uses a voice assistant to control their smart home devices. They can tell the assistant to turn on the lights, adjust the thermostat, and even play music.

AI smart home devices have the potential to revolutionize the way that we live in our homes. By making our homes more convenient, efficient, safe, and accessible, AI smart home devices can improve our quality of life.

Here is a list of AI apps for smart home devices:

- Amazon Alexa
- Google Assistant
- Apple HomeKit
- Samsung SmartThings
- Huawei HiLink
- Xiaomi Mi Home
- Aqara Home
- Tuya Smart
- Smart Life
- IFTTT
- Yonomi
- HomeHabit

- Stringify

These AI apps for smart home devices can be used to control a variety of smart home devices, such as lights, thermostats, locks, cameras, and speakers. They can also be used to create custom automations and routines.

Smart home apps are still under development, but they are already having a major impact on the way that we live in our homes. They are making it possible to control our homes more easily and efficiently, and to create a more personalized and comfortable living environment.

In addition to the above, there are also a number of AI-powered smart home apps that are available for consumers to use on their smartphones and other devices. These apps can be used to control smart home devices, create custom automations, and monitor energy consumption.

AI smart home apps have the potential to revolutionize the way that we live in our homes. By making it possible to control our homes more easily and efficiently, AI smart home apps can make our lives easier and more convenient.

Here are some examples of how AI smart home apps are being used today:

- **People with disabilities**: AI smart home apps are being used by people with disabilities to control their homes and to access information and services that they would not otherwise be able to use. For example, a person who is wheelchair-bound can use an AI smart home app to turn on the lights, adjust the thermostat, and unlock the front door without having to get up.
- **Seniors**: AI smart home apps are being used by seniors to stay independent and to live safely in their own homes.

For example, a senior can use an AI smart home app to set up reminders to take their medication or to call for help in an emergency.

- **Parents**: AI smart home apps are being used by parents to keep their children safe and to manage their household. For example, a parent can use an AI smart home app to lock the doors when they leave the house or to set up a bedtime routine for their children.

AI smart home apps are a powerful tool that can be used for a variety of purposes. They are making it possible for people to control their homes more easily and efficiently, and to create a more personalized and comfortable living environment.

Smart home devices, powered by AI, are transforming how we interact with our living spaces. As technology continues to evolve, these devices will become more intelligent, personalized, and integrated, offering a safer, more convenient, and energy-efficient living experience for users.

9. Social Media Algorithms

Social media algorithms powered by artificial intelligence play a pivotal role in shaping what users see on their feeds, facilitating personalized content delivery and enhancing user engagement. Here's a deeper look into the AI-powered world of social media algorithms.

How Social Media Algorithms Work:

a) Content Ranking and Prioritization:

Description: Social media platforms use AI algorithms to rank and prioritize content on users' feeds. These algorithms consider various factors, such as user engagement history, content type, recency, and relevance, to determine the order in which posts appear.

b) Personalization:

Description: AI analyses user behaviour, including likes, shares, comments, and the types of content interacted with, to personalize content recommendations. Machine learning models predict user preferences and tailor the feed to match individual interests.

c) Content Curation:

Description: AI algorithms curate content by categorizing posts based on themes, topics, or hashtags. This categorization helps in delivering diverse and relevant content to users, ensuring a balanced and engaging experience.

Challenges and Ethical Considerations:

a) Echo Chambers and Filter Bubbles:

Description: Social media algorithms, while personalized, can create echo chambers where users are exposed only to content that aligns with their existing beliefs and opinions. This can reinforce biases and limit diverse perspectives.

b) Misinformation and Fake News:

Description: Social media platforms face challenges in curbing the spread of misinformation and fake news. AI models are deployed to detect and flag false content, but the cat-and-mouse game between algorithms and misinformation creators continues.

c) Algorithmic Bias:

Description: AI algorithms can inadvertently perpetuate biases present in the data they are trained on. This can lead to unfair content distribution, reinforcing stereotypes, and marginalizing certain groups. Ensuring fairness and reducing bias is an ongoing concern.

d) Privacy Concerns:

Description: Personalized content delivery relies on analysing user data. Balancing personalization with user privacy is a challenge, and social media platforms must navigate this delicate balance to maintain user trust.

Applications of AI in Social Media Algorithms:

a) Content Recommendation:

Description: AI algorithms recommend posts, videos, articles, and products based on user preferences and interactions. Content recommendation engines enhance user engagement and keep users on the platform longer.

b) Ad Targeting:

Description: Social media platforms use AI to analyse user data and behaviour to deliver targeted advertisements. Advertisers can specify demographics, interests, and behaviours, allowing for highly tailored ad campaigns that maximize return on investment.

c) Content Moderation:

Description: AI-powered content moderation tools automatically detect and filter out inappropriate, offensive, or harmful content. Machine learning models recognize patterns in text, images, and videos, ensuring a safer environment for users.

d) Sentiment Analysis:

Description: AI algorithms analyse user comments, posts, and interactions to gauge sentiment. Sentiment analysis helps social media platforms understand user emotions, allowing for more empathetic and personalized responses.

Future Trends in Social Media Algorithms:

a) Explainable AI:

Description: Making AI algorithms more transparent and explainable is a growing trend. Users and regulators are demanding greater visibility into how algorithms work and make decisions, ensuring accountability and trust.

b) Combating Deepfakes:

Description: Social media platforms are investing in AI tools to detect and mitigate the impact of deepfake content. Advanced algorithms are essential to identify manipulated media and prevent its dissemination.

c) Enhanced Context Understanding:

Description: AI algorithms are evolving to better understand the context of user posts and interactions. This context-aware understanding helps platforms provide more relevant content and reduce misinterpretation of user intent.

d) Interactive and Immersive Content:

Description: AI-driven interactive content, such as augmented reality (AR) filters and virtual reality (VR) experiences, is becoming popular. AI algorithms enhance these experiences, making them more engaging and dynamic.

AI social media algorithms are helping in a number of ways today, including:

- **Personalization**: AI algorithms are used to personalize the social media experience for each user by recommending content that is likely to be of interest to the user. This is done by analysing the user's past behaviour, such as the posts they have liked, shared, and commented on.

- **Discovery**: AI algorithms help users to discover new content and creators that they might not otherwise have found. This can be done by recommending content based on the user's interests, or by highlighting new and trending content.
- **Engagement**: AI algorithms help to increase user engagement by promoting content that is likely to be popular and interesting to users. This can be done by prioritizing certain types of content, such as videos or images, or by recommending content that is likely to spark conversation.
- **Safety**: AI algorithms are used to detect and remove harmful content from social media platforms. This can include hate speech, misinformation, and spam. AI algorithms can also be used to identify and protect vulnerable users.

Here are some examples of tools that are being used to develop and deploy AI social media algorithms:

- **Machine learning frameworks**: Machine learning frameworks such as TensorFlow, PyTorch, and scikit-learn are used to train and deploy machine learning models.
- **Natural language processing (NLP) tools**: NLP tools are used to process and understand human language. This is essential for developing AI algorithms that can understand and respond to social media posts and comments.
- **Recommendation systems:** Recommendation systems are used to suggest content to users based on their interests and past behaviour.

- **Computer vision tools:** Computer vision tools are used to analyse and understand images and videos. This can be used to develop AI algorithms that can identify objects, people, and scenes in social media posts.

Here are some specific examples of how AI social media algorithms are being used today:

- **Facebook:** Facebook uses AI algorithms to personalize the News Feed for each user, to recommend new friends and groups to join, and to detect and remove harmful content.
- **Instagram:** Instagram uses AI algorithms to recommend new accounts to follow, to identify and promote high-quality content, and to detect and remove harmful content.
- **Twitter**: Twitter uses AI algorithms to personalize the timeline for each user, to recommend trending topics, and to detect and remove harmful content.
- **YouTube**: YouTube uses AI algorithms to recommend new videos to watch, to identify and promote high-quality content, and to detect and remove harmful content.

AI social media algorithms have a number of potential benefits. They can help users to find content that they are likely to be interested in, discover new content and creators, and engage with social media in more meaningful ways. AI algorithms can also help to make social media platforms safer and more inclusive.

However, there are also some potential risks associated with AI social media algorithms. For example, AI algorithms can be used to create echo chambers, where users are only exposed to content that reinforces their existing beliefs. AI algorithms can also be used to manipulate users' emotions and behaviour.

It is important to use AI social media algorithms responsibly and ethically. Social media platforms should be transparent about how they use AI algorithms and should give users control over how their data is used. Users should also be aware of the potential risks of AI social media algorithms and take steps to mitigate them.

Overall, AI social media algorithms have the potential to revolutionize the way that we use social media. However, it is important to use them responsibly and ethically.

Here are some AI apps that are used to power social media algorithms:

- Facebook AI Engine
- Google AI Platform
- Amazon SageMaker
- Microsoft Azure Machine Learning
- IBM Watson Machine Learning
- Clarifai
- Cloudinary
- Kairos
- Face++
- Megvii Face++
- Yitu Technology
- SenseTime

These AI apps are used to train and deploy machine learning models that can analyse user behaviour, social media content, and other data to generate personalized recommendations, predict user engagement, and detect harmful content.

For example, Facebook AI Engine is used to power the company's social media platforms, including Facebook, Instagram, and WhatsApp. It is used to generate personalized recommendations for users, such as who to follow, what to like, and what to watch. It is also used to predict user engagement, such as how likely a user is to click on a link or share a post.

Similarly, Google AI Platform is used to power the company's social media platform, YouTube. It is used to generate personalized recommendations for users, such as what videos to watch and what channels to subscribe to. It is also used to detect harmful content, such as hate speech and violent videos.

AI apps are playing an increasingly important role in social media. They are helping social media platforms to provide more personalized and engaging experiences for their users, and they are also helping to keep social media platforms safe and healthy.

In addition to the above, there are also a number of AI-powered social media analytics apps that are available for businesses and individuals to use. These apps can be used to track social media performance, analyse audience demographics, and identify trends.

AI social media apps have the potential to revolutionize the way that we interact with social media. By making it possible to analyse user behaviour and social media content at scale, AI social media apps can help us to understand social media better and to use it more effectively.

Social media algorithms, powered by AI, continue to evolve to meet user demands for personalized, engaging, and safe online experiences. As technology advances, social media platforms will face the challenge of balancing personalization with privacy, ensuring that algorithms are fair and unbiased, and combating the spread of misinformation and harmful content.

10. Self-Driving Cars

Self-driving cars, also known as autonomous vehicles, utilize a combination of artificial intelligence, machine learning, computer vision, sensor technologies, and advanced algorithms to navigate and operate a vehicle without human intervention. Here's a deeper look into the AI-powered world of self-driving cars.

Components of Self-Driving Cars:

a) Sensors:

Description: Self-driving cars are equipped with various sensors, including LiDAR (Light Detection and Ranging), cameras, radar, ultrasonic sensors, and GPS. These sensors provide real-time data about the vehicle's surroundings, helping the AI system make informed decisions.

b) Perception System:

Description: The perception system processes data from sensors to identify and recognize objects, pedestrians, other vehicles, road signs, lane markings, and obstacles. Computer vision algorithms play a significant role in object detection and classification.

c) Localization:

Description: Localization algorithms use GPS data, maps, and sensor information to determine the vehicle's precise location on the road. High-definition maps help self-driving cars understand lane boundaries and navigate complex intersections.

d) Control System:

Description: The control system uses AI algorithms to process sensor data and determine how the vehicle should respond. It controls steering, acceleration, braking, and other vehicle functions to ensure safe navigation and adherence to traffic rules.

e) Decision-Making and Planning:

Description: AI algorithms analyse sensor data and make real-time decisions based on predefined rules and machine learning models. These decisions involve route planning, lane changes, overtaking, and responding to unexpected events on the road.

Levels of Autonomy:

a) Level 0: No Automation:

Description: The driver is entirely responsible for controlling the vehicle. There is no automation involved.

b) Level 1: Driver Assistance:

Description: The vehicle can assist the driver in specific tasks, such as adaptive cruise control or lane-keeping assistance. However, the driver must remain engaged and vigilant.

c) Level 2: Partial Automation:

Description: The vehicle can control both steering and acceleration/deceleration simultaneously under certain conditions. The driver must be ready to take control when needed.

d) Level 3: Conditional Automation:

Description: The vehicle can handle most driving tasks but may require the driver to intervene in specific situations. The driver can disengage from actively controlling the vehicle in certain conditions.

e) Level 4: High Automation:

Description: The vehicle can perform all driving tasks within specific scenarios or environments without human intervention. However, human control might still be required in certain situations.

f) Level 5: Full Automation:

Description: The vehicle is fully autonomous and can operate under all conditions without any human input. There is no need for a steering wheel or pedals.

Challenges and Considerations:

a) Safety:

Description: Ensuring the safety of self-driving cars is a top priority. AI algorithms must be highly reliable and capable of making split-second decisions to avoid accidents and navigate complex scenarios.

b) Regulations and Legislation:

Description: Developing and implementing regulations for self-driving cars is a complex process. Governments and regulatory bodies worldwide are working to establish standards and guidelines to ensure the safe deployment of autonomous vehicles.

c) Ethical Decisions:

Description: AI systems in self-driving cars might face ethical dilemmas, such as how to prioritize the safety of the occupants versus pedestrians in certain situations. Resolving these ethical challenges is an ongoing area of research.

d) Data Security and Privacy:

Description: Self-driving cars generate vast amounts of data. Ensuring the security and privacy of this data, including location information and sensor data, is crucial to protect users' privacy and prevent unauthorized access.

Future Trends in Self-Driving Cars:

a) Connected and Cooperative Driving:

Description: Self-driving cars will communicate with each other and with infrastructure elements such as traffic signals and road signs. Cooperative driving technologies will enhance safety and traffic flow.

b) Enhanced Sensor Technologies:

Description: Advances in sensor technologies, including improved LiDAR and radar systems, will enhance the perception capabilities of self-driving cars, allowing them to navigate complex and dynamic environments more effectively.

c) AI for Human-Vehicle Interaction:

Description: AI systems will play a significant role in human-vehicle interaction, enabling natural language communication and understanding passengers' preferences and needs. Personalized in-car experiences will become more prevalent.

d) Urban Mobility Solutions:

Description: Self-driving cars will be integrated into broader urban mobility solutions, including ride-sharing, autonomous shuttles, and on-demand transportation services. These systems will contribute to more efficient and sustainable urban transportation.

AI self-driving cars are helping in a number of ways today, including:

- **Improving safety**: AI self-driving cars have the potential to significantly improve road safety by reducing the number of accidents caused by human error. For example, AI self-driving cars are better able to perceive their surroundings and to predict the behaviour of other objects in the environment than human drivers.
- **Reducing traffic congestion**: AI self-driving cars can help to reduce traffic congestion by communicating with each other and coordinating their movements. For example, AI self-driving cars can form platoons, which are groups of cars that travel closely together to reduce drag and improve fuel efficiency.

- **Increasing accessibility**: AI self-driving cars can help to increase accessibility to transportation for people with disabilities and seniors. For example, people who are unable to drive themselves can use AI self-driving cars to get around independently.
- **Creating new economic opportunities**: AI self-driving cars are creating new economic opportunities in areas such as transportation, logistics, and delivery. For example, AI self-driving trucks can be used to transport goods more efficiently and cheaply, and AI self-driving cars can be used to deliver food and groceries to customers' doorsteps.

Here are some examples of tools that are being used to develop and deploy AI self-driving cars:

- **Sensors**: AI self-driving cars use a variety of sensors to perceive their surroundings, including cameras, radar, and lidar. These sensors generate a large amount of data that must be processed in real time by the car's AI system.
- **Machine learning algorithms**: AI self-driving cars use machine learning algorithms to train and deploy models that can identify objects in the environment, predict the behaviour of other objects in the environment, and make decisions about how to navigate safely.
- **Simulation platforms**: AI self-driving cars are tested and validated in simulation platforms before they are deployed on the road. Simulation platforms allow developers to test different scenarios and to identify and fix potential problems in a safe and controlled environment.

AI self-driving cars are still under development, but they have the potential to revolutionize the way that we travel. AI self-driving cars can make our roads safer, reduce traffic congestion, increase accessibility to transportation, and create new economic opportunities.

Here are some AI apps that are used to power self-driving cars:

- NVIDIA Drive Hyperion
- Mobileye Drive
- Argo AI
- Aurora
- Waymo Driver
- TuSimple
- Cruise Origin
- Kodiak Robotics
- Nuro
- Pony.ai
- WeRide
- AutoX

These AI apps use a variety of machine learning algorithms to perceive the environment around the car, make decisions about how to navigate, and control the car's steering, braking, and acceleration.

For example, NVIDIA Drive Hyperion is a self-driving car platform that uses a variety of sensors, including cameras, radar, and lidar, to generate a 360-degree view of the car's surroundings. The platform then uses machine learning algorithms to identify objects in the environment, such as other vehicles, pedestrians, and traffic signs. The platform also uses machine learning algorithms to predict the behaviour of other objects in the environment and to make decisions about how to navigate safely.

Similarly, Mobileye Drive is a self-driving car platform that uses a variety of sensors, including cameras, radar, and lidar, to generate a 360-degree view of the car's surroundings. The platform then uses machine learning algorithms to identify objects in the environment and to predict the behaviour of other objects in the environment. The platform also uses machine learning algorithms to make decisions about how to navigate safely.

AI apps are playing an increasingly important role in self-driving cars. They are helping to make self-driving cars safer and more reliable.

In addition to the above, there are also a number of AI-powered self-driving car simulation platforms that are available for developers and researchers to use. These platforms can be used to test and validate self-driving car software in a safe and controlled environment.

AI self-driving apps have the potential to revolutionize the way that we travel. By making it possible for cars to drive themselves, AI self-driving apps can make our lives easier and safer.

Self-driving cars represent a transformative technology with the potential to revolutionize transportation, enhance road safety, and increase mobility for people with disabilities or limited access to transportation. Ongoing research and advancements in AI and related technologies continue to shape the future of autonomous vehicles.

11. Medical Diagnosis

AI in medical diagnosis refers to the use of artificial intelligence techniques, including machine learning and deep learning, to assist healthcare professionals in diagnosing diseases and conditions. These technologies analyse medical data, such as images, test results, and patient histories, to provide accurate and timely diagnostic insights. Here's a deeper look into the AI-powered world of medical diagnosis.

Types of Medical Data Analysed by AI:

a) Medical Imaging:

Description: AI algorithms analyse medical images such as X-rays, CT scans, MRI scans, and histopathology slides. Deep learning models, particularly convolutional neural networks (CNNs), excel in image recognition tasks and are used for detecting abnormalities and tumours.

b) Genomic Data:

Description: AI analyses genomic data to identify genetic variations associated with diseases. This information is crucial for diagnosing genetic disorders, predicting disease risk, and personalizing treatment plans, a field known as genomic medicine.

c) Clinical Notes and Electronic Health Records (EHR):

Description: AI processes unstructured clinical notes and structured EHR data to extract relevant information. Natural language processing (NLP) algorithms analyse textual data, enabling healthcare providers to identify patterns, track patient histories, and assist in diagnosis.

d) Biomedical Signals:

Description: AI analyses physiological signals such as electrocardiograms (ECG), electroencephalograms (EEG), and vital signs. Machine learning models detect anomalies in these signals, aiding in the diagnosis of heart conditions, neurological disorders, and other medical issues.

Applications of AI in Medical Diagnosis:

a) Disease Detection and Diagnosis:

Description: AI algorithms analyse medical data to detect diseases such as cancer, diabetes, cardiovascular disorders, and neurological conditions. Machine learning models learn from labelled data to identify patterns and abnormalities, assisting physicians in accurate and early diagnosis.

b) Radiology and Imaging Diagnosis:

Description: AI-powered image analysis assists radiologists in detecting and characterizing abnormalities in medical images. Deep learning models highlight areas of concern, speeding up the diagnosis process and reducing the chances of oversight.

c) Pathology and Histopathology:

Description: AI algorithms analyse pathology slides to identify cancerous cells and other abnormalities. This technology, known as digital pathology, enhances the accuracy and efficiency of histopathological diagnoses.

d) Risk Prediction and Prognosis:

Description: AI analyses patient data to predict disease risk and prognosis. Machine learning models consider various factors, such as genetic markers, lifestyle choices, and environmental factors, to assess a patient's risk of developing specific conditions and predict disease outcomes.

e) Infectious Disease Diagnosis:

Description: AI assists in diagnosing infectious diseases by analysing symptoms, patient history, and laboratory test results. AI models can help healthcare professionals identify outbreaks, track the spread of diseases, and make data-driven decisions in epidemic situations.

Challenges and Considerations:

a) Data Quality and Bias:

Description: AI models heavily depend on the quality and diversity of the training data. Biased or incomplete datasets can lead to biased predictions. Ensuring representative and high-quality data is crucial for accurate and fair diagnoses.

b) Interpretability and Trust:

Description: AI models, particularly deep learning models, are often considered "black boxes" because their decision-making processes are complex and hard to interpret. Building transparent and interpretable AI systems is a challenge for medical diagnosis.

c) Regulatory Compliance and Ethical Concerns:

Description: AI applications in healthcare must comply with regulatory standards and privacy regulations such as HIPAA in the United States. Ethical considerations, including patient consent, data privacy, and algorithmic fairness, are paramount in medical AI.

d) Integration with Clinical Workflow:

Description: AI tools need to seamlessly integrate into the existing clinical workflow to be effective. User-friendly interfaces and integration with electronic health record systems are essential for adoption by healthcare professionals.

Future Trends in AI Medical Diagnosis:

a) Explainable AI in Healthcare:

Description: Developing AI models that are explainable and interpretable is a significant area of research. Explainable AI helps healthcare professionals understand and trust AI-generated diagnoses, leading to more informed decisions.

b) Federated Learning:

Description: Federated learning allows AI models to be trained across multiple institutions without sharing patient data. This approach enhances privacy and security while enabling collaborative research and model development.

c) AI-Driven Drug Discovery:

Description: AI accelerates drug discovery by analysing vast biological datasets and predicting potential drug candidates. Machine learning models identify molecular interactions, predict drug-target interactions, and optimize drug compounds, leading to faster drug development processes.

d) Continuous Monitoring and Personalized Medicine:

Description: AI-powered wearable devices and continuous monitoring systems collect real-time health data. Machine learning algorithms analyse this data to detect early signs of disease, predict exacerbations, and provide personalized treatment recommendations.

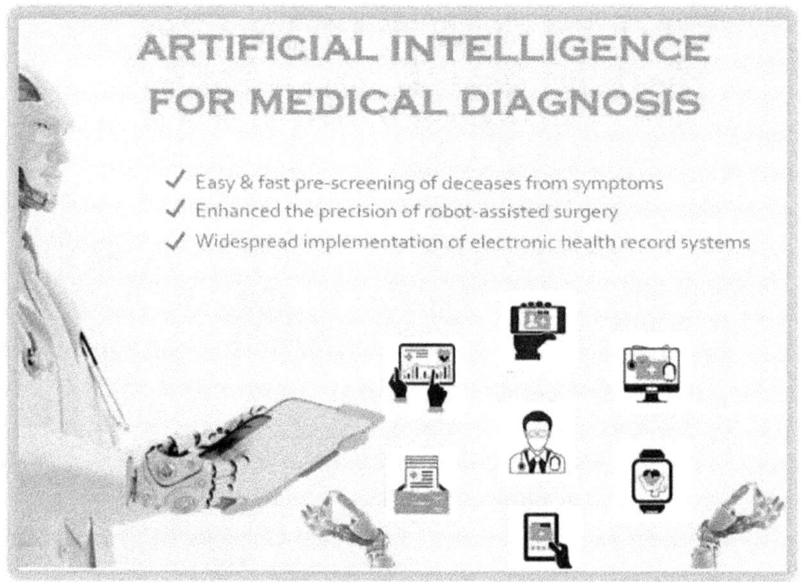

AI medical diagnosis is helping in a number of ways today, including:

- Improving the accuracy of diagnosis: AI algorithms can analyse large amounts of data to identify patterns and abnormalities that may indicate disease. This can help doctors to diagnose diseases more accurately, especially in cases where the symptoms are complex or subtle.

- Personalizing diagnosis and treatment: AI can be used to personalize diagnosis and treatment by taking into account the patient's individual medical history, genetic makeup, and other factors. This can help to improve the outcomes of treatment and to reduce the risk of side effects.
- Making healthcare more accessible: AI-powered diagnostic tools can be used to provide healthcare in remote and underserved areas. This can help to improve access to healthcare for people who may not have access to traditional medical services.

Here are some examples of AI tools that are being used for medical diagnosis today:

- Deep learning models: Deep learning models are a type of AI algorithm that can be trained to identify patterns and abnormalities in medical images, such as X-rays, MRI scans, and CT scans. Deep learning models have been shown to be very accurate at diagnosing a variety of diseases, including cancer, heart disease, and Alzheimer's disease.
- Natural language processing (NLP) tools: NLP tools can be used to extract information from medical records, such as laboratory results, patient notes, and imaging reports. This information can then be used to train AI algorithms to diagnose diseases and to recommend treatments.
- Clinical decision support systems (CDSS): CDSS are computer systems that provide doctors with information and alerts to help them make better decisions about patient care. CDSS can use AI to analyze patient data and to generate recommendations for diagnosis and treatment.

Here are some specific examples of how AI medical diagnosis is being used today:

- A radiologist uses a deep learning model to diagnose lung cancer on X-rays more accurately and quickly than human radiologists.
- A pathologist uses an AI-powered microscope to identify cancer cells in tissue samples.
- A dermatologist uses an AI-powered app to diagnose skin conditions more accurately than human dermatologists.
- A doctor uses a CDSS to get recommendations for diagnosing and treating a patient with a complex medical history.

AI medical diagnosis is a rapidly developing field, and new tools and applications are being developed all the time. As AI technology continues to improve, we can expect to see even more ways that AI can be used to improve the accuracy, personalization, and accessibility of healthcare.

It is important to note that AI medical diagnosis tools are not perfect, and they should not be used as a substitute for the judgment of a qualified healthcare professional. However, AI medical diagnosis tools can be a valuable tool for doctors to use in conjunction with their own experience and expertise.

Here are some AI apps names for medical diagnosis:

- Babylon Health
- Buoy Health
- Cardiogram
- DermCheck
- HealthTap
- IBM Watson for Oncology

- iTriage
- K Health
- LiveHealth Online
- MDacne
- Mediktor
- MyChart
- MySymptoms
- Parsley Health
- PlushCare
- SkinVision
- Teladoc Health
- TytoCare
- WebMD Symptom Checker
- Zocdoc

These apps use AI to analyze symptoms, medical history, and other factors to provide users with a diagnosis or to recommend further medical attention. It is important to note that these apps are not a substitute for medical advice from a qualified healthcare professional.

In addition to the above, there are many other AI-powered medical diagnosis tools that are being developed and used by healthcare professionals. For example, AI algorithms are being used to develop new ways to detect cancer, heart disease, and other diseases from medical images and data. AI is also being used to develop new clinical decision support systems that can help doctors to make better decisions about patient care.

AI is rapidly transforming the field of medical diagnosis. As AI technology continues to improve, we can expect to see even more innovative and effective ways to use AI to improve the accuracy, personalization, and accessibility of healthcare.

AI in medical diagnosis is revolutionizing healthcare by enhancing diagnostic accuracy, improving patient outcomes, and enabling more efficient healthcare delivery. Ongoing research and collaboration between healthcare professionals and data scientists continue to drive innovation in this critical field.

12. Code Generation

AI-powered code generation refers to the use of artificial intelligence techniques, particularly machine learning and natural language processing, to automatically generate code snippets, algorithms, or even entire software applications. This technology assists developers in various programming tasks, speeding up the development process and reducing the likelihood of errors. Here's a deeper look into the AI-powered world of code generation.

Types of Code Generation:

a) Code Completion:

Description: AI-powered code completion tools suggest code snippets or entire lines of code as developers' type. These suggestions are based on context, libraries, and patterns, improving coding efficiency and accuracy.

b) Code Summarization:

Description: AI algorithms generate summaries for code snippets or functions. These summaries provide a concise understanding of the code's functionality, making it easier for developers to comprehend complex codebases.

c) Code Translation:

Description: AI translates code from one programming language to another. This is particularly useful when developers need to port applications to different platforms or rewrite code in a language better suited for a specific task.

d) Code Refactoring:

Description: AI-powered tools analyse existing codebases and suggest improvements, such as renaming variables, extracting functions, or optimizing algorithms. Code refactoring enhances code readability, maintainability, and performance.

e) Low-Code and No-Code Development:

Description: AI platforms enable non-technical users to create applications using visual interfaces and predefined modules. These platforms automatically generate underlying code based on user interactions, simplifying the development process for individuals with limited programming skills.

How AI Generates Code:

a) Natural Language Processing (NLP):

Description: NLP models understand human-written instructions and queries. When developers provide high-level descriptions of the desired functionality, NLP-based code generation tools translate these descriptions into code snippets, leveraging predefined templates and patterns.

b) Machine Learning Models:

Description: Machine learning algorithms, particularly recurrent neural networks (RNNs) and transformers, learn from vast amounts of code to predict the next tokens or characters in a code sequence. These models generate code by predicting the syntax and structure based on the provided context.

c) Code Templates and Patterns:

Description: AI-powered code generation tools often use templates and predefined patterns for common programming tasks. By recognizing the context, these tools fill in the missing code components, allowing developers to focus on high-level logic and architecture.

Challenges and Considerations:

a) Quality and Correctness:

Description: Ensuring generated code is of high quality, follows best practices, and is bug-free is a challenge. AI models need rigorous testing and validation to produce reliable code that performs as intended.

b) Context Understanding:

Description: AI models must accurately understand the developer's intent and context. Ambiguous descriptions or incomplete instructions can lead to code generation errors. Improving context understanding is an ongoing area of research.

c) Security Concerns:

Description: Generated code must not introduce security vulnerabilities or malicious intents. Ensuring that AI-generated code is secure and adheres to security best practices is essential to prevent potential threats.

d) Maintainability:

Description: While AI can generate code quickly, ensuring that the generated code is maintainable in the long run is crucial. Developers need to understand and modify the generated code without difficulty.

Future Trends in Code Generation:

a) Multimodal AI:

Description: Integrating text-based instructions with other modalities, such as diagrams, images, or even voice, enhances the understanding of developer intent. Multimodal AI systems can generate code based on a combination of textual and visual inputs.

b) Contextual Code Generation:

Description: Future AI systems will focus on understanding complex contexts and generating code that adapts to specific project requirements, coding styles, and frameworks. Contextual code generation aims to provide highly tailored and context-aware solutions.

c) Collaborative Coding:

Description: AI tools will support collaborative coding environments, enabling multiple developers to work together seamlessly. These tools will assist in code synchronization, conflict resolution, and real-time collaboration, improving team productivity.

d) Domain-Specific Code Generation:

Description: AI models will be specialized for specific domains, such as web development, data science, or mobile app development. These domain-specific models will generate code optimized for the requirements and constraints of the respective domains.

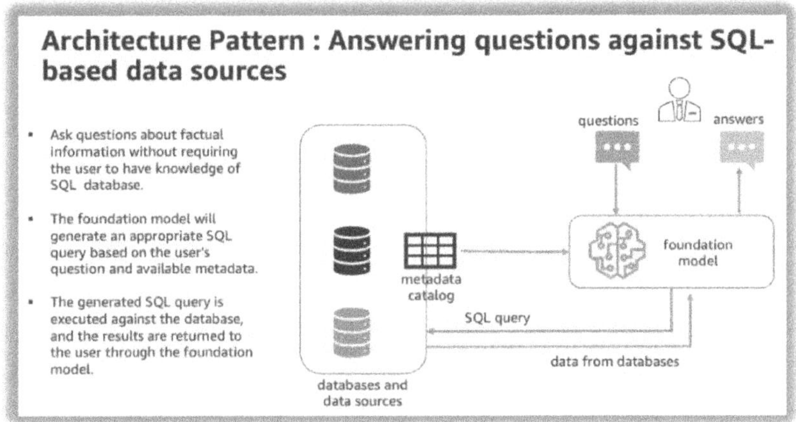

AI code generation is helping in a number of ways today, including:

- Improving programmer productivity: AI code generation tools can help programmers to write code more quickly and efficiently by automating repetitive tasks and suggesting code snippets. This can free up programmers to focus on more complex and creative tasks.
- Improving code quality: AI code generation tools can help programmers to write better code by identifying potential errors and suggesting improvements. This can help to reduce the number of bugs in software and to improve the overall quality of software development.
- Making programming more accessible: AI code generation tools can make programming more accessible to people with no prior coding experience. This can help to democratize programming and to create a more diverse pool of software developers.

Here are some examples of AI code generation tools:

- GitHub Copilot: GitHub Copilot is a VS Code extension that uses AI to suggest code snippets, complete functions, and even generate entire files.
- TabNine: TabNine is a code editor extension that uses AI to suggest code completions, refactorings, and other helpful features.
- Kite: Kite is a code completion tool that uses AI to suggest relevant code snippets based on the context of the code being edited.
- Coderunner: Coderunner is a code generation tool that can be used to generate code in a variety of programming languages based on natural language descriptions.
- DeepCode: DeepCode is a code review tool that uses AI to identify potential errors and security vulnerabilities in code.

Here are some specific examples of how AI code generation is being used today:

- A programmer uses GitHub Copilot to generate a function that performs a complex data transformation task. This saves the programmer hours of time and helps to reduce the risk of errors.
- A software development team uses TabNine to identify and fix potential bugs in their code. This helps to improve the quality of their code and to release bug-free software to their customers.
- A student uses Coderunner to generate a simple program to solve a math problem. This helps the student to learn programming and to solve the math problem more efficiently.
- A company uses DeepCode to review their code for potential security vulnerabilities before deploying it to

production. This helps to protect the company from cyberattacks.

AI code generation is a rapidly developing field, and new tools and applications are being developed all the time. As AI technology continues to improve, we can expect to see even more ways that AI can be used to improve the productivity, quality, and accessibility of software development.

Here are some AI apps names for code generation:

- GitHub Copilot
- TabNine
- Kite
- Coderunner
- DeepCode
- Copilot.ai
- PolyCoder
- CodeWhisperer
- Replit
- Stack Overflow Copilot
- Amazon CodeWhisperer
- AI Assistant for Programming
- Probot

These apps use AI to generate code in a variety of programming languages, such as Python, Java, JavaScript, C++, and Go. They can be used to generate code snippets, complete functions, and even entire files.

In addition to the above, there are many other AI-powered code generation tools that are being developed and used by software developers. For example, AI algorithms are being used to develop new ways to generate code from natural language descriptions, to translate code from one language to another, and to identify and fix potential bugs in code.

AI is rapidly transforming the field of code generation. As AI technology continues to improve, we can expect to see even more innovative and effective ways to use AI to improve the productivity, quality, and accessibility of software development.

It is important to note that AI code generation tools are not a substitute for the knowledge and skills of a software developer. However, AI code generation tools can be a valuable tool for software developers to use in conjunction with their own expertise.

AI-powered code generation continues to evolve, shaping the way developers create software. As these technologies advance, they have the potential to revolutionize software development by increasing productivity, enabling faster prototyping, and democratizing access to coding expertise. Ongoing research and innovation in AI-driven code generation will continue to redefine the landscape of software engineering.

13. Robotic Process Automation

Robotic Process Automation (RPA) refers to the use of software robots or "bots" that mimic human actions to automate repetitive and rule-based tasks within business processes. Artificial Intelligence (AI) plays a significant role in enhancing RPA capabilities, making automation more intelligent, adaptive, and efficient. Here's a deeper look into the AI-powered world of Robotic Process Automation.

Components of RPA with AI:

a) Machine Learning:

Description: Machine learning algorithms in RPA enable bots to learn from data, identify patterns, and make predictions. ML models can be used for tasks like data extraction, document classification, sentiment analysis, and decision-making, making automation smarter and more context-aware.

b) Natural Language Processing (NLP):

Description: NLP allows bots to understand and process human language. Bots equipped with NLP capabilities can interact with users, extract information from unstructured text, and automate tasks based on textual data, enhancing communication and information processing.

c) Computer Vision:

Description: Computer vision technology enables bots to "see" and interpret visual information from the screen just like a human. It's used for tasks such as reading data from images, recognizing objects, and automating processes that involve interacting with graphical user interfaces (GUIs).

d) Cognitive Automation:

Description: Cognitive automation combines various AI technologies to enable bots to mimic human cognition. This includes understanding complex instructions, reasoning, and decision-making. Cognitive automation enhances bots' ability to handle tasks that require advanced problem-solving skills.

Applications of AI in RPA:

a) Data Extraction and Processing:

Description: AI algorithms extract data from diverse sources, including emails, documents, PDFs, and images. ML models identify patterns and extract relevant information, reducing manual data entry and improving accuracy.

b) Document Classification and Recognition:

Description: NLP and computer vision technologies classify documents, extract meaningful data, and recognize structured and unstructured content. Bots can process invoices, receipts, forms, and emails more efficiently using these AI capabilities.

c) Chatbots and Virtual Assistants:

Description: RPA integrated with AI-powered chatbots and virtual assistants enables intelligent automation of customer interactions. These bots can understand user queries, provide relevant responses, and automate tasks based on user requests.

d) Predictive Analytics and Decision-Making:

Description: Machine learning algorithms analyse historical data to make predictions and informed decisions. Bots equipped with predictive analytics capabilities can optimize processes, forecast demand, and make data-driven decisions in real-time.

e) Compliance and Risk Management:

Description: AI algorithms monitor transactions and data patterns to detect anomalies and potential risks. RPA bots, coupled with AI, can automate compliance checks, identify fraudulent activities, and ensure adherence to regulations and policies.

Challenges and Considerations:

a) Integration Complexity:

Description: Integrating AI technologies with RPA systems requires careful planning and integration efforts. Ensuring seamless communication between different components is essential for effective automation.

b) Data Quality and Accuracy:

Description: AI models heavily depend on the quality of training data. Noisy or biased data can lead to inaccurate predictions. Data cleansing and validation are crucial to maintaining high accuracy levels in AI-powered RPA.

c) Ethical and Regulatory Considerations:

Description: RPA with AI raises ethical concerns related to privacy, data security, and algorithmic fairness. Ensuring compliance with regulations such as GDPR and addressing biases in AI models are critical considerations.

d) Human-AI Collaboration:

Description: Determining the right balance between automation and human intervention is essential. Certain tasks may require human judgment or empathy, and understanding when to involve humans is crucial for successful RPA implementation.

Future Trends in AI-powered RPA:

a) Hyper automation:

Description: Hyper automation involves integrating RPA with AI, machine learning, and other advanced technologies to automate end-to-end business processes. It aims to automate not just repetitive tasks but entire business workflows, enhancing efficiency and productivity.

b) Explainable AI in RPA:

Description: Developing AI models that are explainable and transparent is crucial. In RPA, understanding how AI algorithms make decisions is essential for ensuring accountability, compliance, and user trust.

c) AI-Driven Process Discovery:

Description: AI-powered tools analyse user interactions and identify repetitive tasks, bottlenecks, and inefficiencies in business processes. This analysis helps organizations prioritize automation opportunities and optimize their processes.

d) Intelligent Document Processing (IDP):

Description: IDP combines OCR (Optical Character Recognition) with NLP and machine learning to extract and understand data from documents. AI-powered IDP systems automate document processing tasks, such as invoice processing and contract management, with high accuracy.

AI for robotic process automation (RPA) is helping in a number of ways today, including:

- Expanding the range of tasks that can be automated: AI can help to automate a wider range of tasks than traditional RPA tools, including tasks that are complex, unstructured, or judgment-based. This is because AI can learn and adapt to new tasks and situations, and it can make decisions based on data and information.
- Improving the accuracy and efficiency of automation: AI can help to improve the accuracy and efficiency of automation by identifying and correcting errors, and by automating repetitive tasks more effectively. This can

help businesses to save time and money, and to improve the quality of their operations.

- Making automation more accessible: AI can make automation more accessible to businesses of all sizes by providing affordable and easy-to-use tools. This is because AI-powered RPA tools are often cloud-based and do not require a large upfront investment in hardware or software.

Here are some examples of how AI for RPA is being used today:

- A bank uses AI-powered RPA to automate the process of opening new bank accounts. This helps the bank to reduce the amount of time it takes to open new accounts and to improve the customer experience.
- A healthcare provider uses AI-powered RPA to automate the process of processing insurance claims. This helps the healthcare provider to reduce the amount of time it takes to process claims and to get patients reimbursed for their medical expenses more quickly.
- A manufacturing company uses AI-powered RPA to automate the process of quality control. This helps the company to reduce the number of defects in its products and to improve the quality of its goods.

Here are some specific examples of AI tools that are being used for RPA today:

- UiPath: UiPath is a leading RPA platform that offers a variety of AI-powered features, such as AI-powered document processing, AI-powered decision making, and AI-powered process mining.
- Automation Anywhere: Automation Anywhere is another leading RPA platform that offers a variety of AI-powered

features, such as AI-powered data extraction, AI-powered analytics, and AI-powered process discovery.

- Blue Prism: Blue Prism is a leading RPA platform that offers a variety of AI-powered features, such as AI-powered document understanding, AI-powered cognitive automation, and AI-powered process intelligence.

AI for RPA is a rapidly developing field, and new tools and applications are being developed all the time. As AI technology continues to improve, we can expect to see even more ways that AI can be used to improve the scope, accuracy, efficiency, and accessibility of RPA.

It is important to note that AI for RPA is not a replacement for human workers. However, AI for RPA can help businesses to automate tasks more effectively and to free up their employees to focus on more strategic and creative work.

Here are some AI apps names for robotic process automation (RPA):

- UiPath
- Automation Anywhere
- Blue Prism
- WorkFusion
- Microsoft Power Automate
- Pega
- NICE Robotic Process Automation
- Kofax RPA
- Redwood Software

- Antworks RPA
- Kryon RPA
- Appian RPA
- Softomotive WinAutomation

These apps use AI to automate a wide range of tasks, such as data entry, order processing, customer service, and IT support. They can be used to automate tasks on a variety of platforms, including Windows, Mac, and Linux.

In addition to the above, there are many other AI-powered RPA tools that are being developed and used by businesses of all sizes. As AI technology continues to improve, we can expect to see even more innovative and effective ways to use AI for RPA.

It is important to note that AI for RPA is not a replacement for human workers. However, AI for RPA can help businesses to automate tasks more effectively and to free up their employees to focus on more strategic and creative work.

AI-powered RPA continues to transform businesses by automating complex tasks and enabling organizations to focus on high-value activities. As technology advances, the integration of AI in RPA will become more sophisticated, driving increased efficiency and innovation in various industries.

14. Predictive Analytics

Predictive analytics is a field of data analysis that uses various statistical algorithms, machine learning techniques, and AI models to identify the likelihood of future outcomes based on historical data. It enables organizations to make data-driven decisions, anticipate trends, and forecast future events. Here's a deeper look into the AI-powered world of predictive analytics.

Components of Predictive Analytics with AI:

a) Data Collection and Preparation:

Description: Predictive analytics starts with collecting relevant data from various sources. AI algorithms assist in cleaning, preprocessing, and transforming raw data into a usable format. Natural Language Processing (NLP) can be used to extract insights from unstructured text data.

b) Feature Selection and Engineering:

Description: AI models help in identifying the most relevant features (variables) from the dataset. Feature engineering techniques create new meaningful features from existing data, improving the accuracy and effectiveness of predictive models.

c) Algorithms and Models:

Description: AI algorithms, including regression, decision trees, neural networks, and ensemble methods, are employed for predictive modelling. Deep learning models, especially recurrent neural networks (RNNs) and transformers, are used for sequence prediction tasks, such as time series forecasting and natural language processing tasks.

d) Evaluation and Validation:

Description: AI techniques like cross-validation and bootstrapping are used to assess the performance of predictive models. Metrics such as accuracy, precision, recall, and F1-score are used to evaluate the model's effectiveness.

Applications of Predictive Analytics with AI:

a) Financial Forecasting:

Description: Predictive analytics, powered by AI, helps in forecasting stock prices, currency exchange rates, and market trends. Machine learning models analyse historical trading data and news sentiment to predict market movements.

b) Customer Churn Prediction:

Description: AI models analyse customer behaviour data to predict the likelihood of customers leaving a service or subscription. This insight allows businesses to take proactive measures to retain customers, such as personalized offers or customer engagement initiatives.

c) Healthcare Predictive Analytics:

Description: Predictive analytics in healthcare uses AI to predict disease outbreaks, patient readmissions, and potential complications. Machine learning models analyse patient data to predict disease risks, enabling preventive interventions and personalized treatment plans.

d) Supply Chain Optimization:

Description: Predictive analytics optimizes supply chain operations by forecasting demand, predicting supplier performance, and identifying potential disruptions. AI algorithms analyse historical data and external factors to improve inventory management and reduce costs.

e) Predictive Maintenance:

Description: In industries like manufacturing and transportation, predictive analytics powered by AI predicts when equipment or vehicles are likely to fail. Machine learning models analyse sensor data to detect patterns indicating potential breakdowns, allowing for timely maintenance and reducing downtime.

Challenges and Considerations:

a) Data Quality and Availability:

Description: The accuracy of predictive models heavily depends on the quality and completeness of the data. Noisy or biased data can lead to inaccurate predictions. Additionally, ensuring data privacy and security is crucial when dealing with sensitive information.

b) Interpretability and Explainability:

Description: Complex AI models, especially deep learning models, can be difficult to interpret. In critical applications such as healthcare and finance, understanding how a model arrived at a particular prediction is essential for user trust and regulatory compliance.

c) Scalability and Deployment:

Description: Deploying predictive models at scale, especially in real-time applications, requires efficient algorithms and infrastructure. Ensuring that AI models can handle large volumes of data and provide predictions in real time is a challenge.

d) Ethical Considerations:

Description: Predictive analytics can inadvertently perpetuate biases present in the data. Ensuring fairness and mitigating biases in predictive models is an ongoing concern. Ethical considerations also include transparency in how predictive analytics is used, especially in sensitive applications like hiring and lending.

Future Trends in Predictive Analytics with AI:

a) Automated Machine Learning (AutoML):

Description: AutoML platforms automate the process of selecting, training, and deploying machine learning models. These platforms enable users with limited data science expertise to leverage predictive analytics, democratizing AI technology.

b) Explainable AI:

Description: Making AI models more interpretable and explainable is a growing trend. Explainable AI techniques help users, including non-experts, understand how predictive models make decisions, enhancing transparency and user trust.

c) Anomaly Detection and Outlier Analysis:

Description: AI-powered anomaly detection techniques identify unusual patterns or events in data. These methods are valuable for fraud detection, cybersecurity, and quality control, allowing organizations to proactively address irregularities.

d) Time Series Forecasting with AI:

Description: Advanced AI models, particularly deep learning architectures like Long Short-Term Memory (LSTM) networks, are increasingly being used for accurate time series forecasting. These models excel in predicting sequences of data points, making them valuable for applications like demand forecasting and financial forecasting.

AI for predictive analytics is helping in a number of ways today, including:

- Improving business decision-making: AI-powered predictive analytics tools can help businesses to make better decisions about their products, services, and operations. For example, AI can be used to predict customer demand, forecast sales, and identify potential risks.

- Reducing costs and improving efficiency: AI-powered predictive analytics tools can help businesses to reduce costs and improve efficiency by automating tasks, such as fraud detection and preventive maintenance.
- Creating new opportunities: AI-powered predictive analytics tools can help businesses to create new opportunities by identifying trends and patterns that would be difficult to see with the naked eye. For example, AI can be used to identify new customer segments, develop new products, and expand into new markets.

Here are some examples of how AI for predictive analytics is being used today:

- A retailer uses AI-powered predictive analytics to forecast customer demand and optimize its inventory levels. This helps the retailer to avoid stockouts and to reduce its inventory costs.
- A financial services company uses AI-powered predictive analytics to detect fraud and to prevent money laundering. This helps the company to protect its customers and to avoid financial losses.
- A manufacturing company uses AI-powered predictive analytics to identify potential equipment failures and to schedule preventive maintenance. This helps the company to avoid production downtime and to reduce its maintenance costs.

Here are some specific examples of AI tools that are being used for predictive analytics today:

- Google Cloud AI Platform: Google Cloud AI Platform offers a variety of AI services that can be used for predictive analytics, such as Google Cloud Prediction

API, Google Cloud AutoML, and Google Cloud Dataproc.

- Amazon Web Services (AWS): AWS offers a variety of AI services that can be used for predictive analytics, such as Amazon SageMaker, Amazon Comprehend, and Amazon Forecast.
- Microsoft Azure: Azure offers a variety of AI services that can be used for predictive analytics, such as Azure Machine Learning Studio, Azure Cognitive Services, and Azure HDInsight.

AI for predictive analytics is a rapidly developing field, and new tools and applications are being developed all the time. As AI technology continues to improve, we can expect to see even more ways that AI can be used to improve the accuracy, efficiency, and impact of predictive analytics.

It is important to note that AI for predictive analytics is not a magic bullet. It is important to have high-quality data and to use AI tools responsibly. However, AI for predictive analytics can be a powerful tool for businesses to make better decisions, reduce costs, and create new opportunities.

Here are some AI apps names for predictive analytics:

- Alteryx
- Dataiku
- H2O.ai
- IBM SPSS
- KNIME Analytics Platform
- Microsoft Azure Machine Learning Studio

- RapidMiner
- SAS Visual Analytics
- Sisense
- Tableau
- ThoughtSpot
- Yellowbrick Data Warehouse

These apps use AI to analyse data and identify trends and patterns that can be used to make predictions about the future. They can be used by businesses of all sizes to improve their decision-making, reduce costs, and create new opportunities.

In addition to the above, there are many other AI-powered predictive analytics tools that are being developed and used by businesses and organizations today. As AI technology continues to improve, we can expect to see even more innovative and effective ways to use AI for predictive analytics.

It is important to note that AI for predictive analytics is not a replacement for human analysts. However, AI tools can help analysts to work more efficiently and effectively by automating tasks and providing insights that would be difficult to see with the naked eye.

Predictive analytics, combined with AI, continues to revolutionize decision-making across various industries. As AI technologies advance, predictive analytics will become more sophisticated, enabling organizations to gain deeper insights, make more accurate predictions, and optimize their operations for enhanced efficiency and competitiveness.

15. Customer Service

Artificial Intelligence (AI) is transforming customer service by enhancing efficiency, personalization, and overall customer experience. AI-powered customer service solutions utilize various technologies, including Natural Language Processing (NLP), chatbots, virtual assistants, sentiment analysis, and machine learning algorithms, to automate processes and provide intelligent responses to customer queries. Here's a deeper look into the AI-powered world of customer service.

Components of AI in Customer Service:

a) Chatbots and Virtual Assistants:

Description: Chatbots and virtual assistants are AI-driven tools that engage with customers in natural language conversations. They handle routine queries, provide product information, assist with troubleshooting, and even process transactions, providing instant responses to customers' inquiries.

b) Sentiment Analysis:

Description: Sentiment analysis algorithms analyse customer interactions, such as emails, social media posts, and chat messages, to determine the emotional tone and sentiment expressed. This information helps businesses gauge customer satisfaction, identify issues, and respond effectively.

c) Predictive Analytics:

Description: Predictive analytics in customer service utilizes AI models to forecast customer behaviour, preferences, and needs. By analysing historical data, businesses can anticipate customer demands, personalize offerings, and proactively address customer concerns.

d) Voice Assistants:

Description: Voice assistants, like Amazon Alexa and Google Assistant, use AI to understand spoken language. They enable hands-free interactions, allowing customers to inquire about products, services, or appointments using voice commands.

Applications of AI in Customer Service:

a) Automated Customer Support:

Description: AI-powered chatbots handle a wide range of customer queries, such as FAQs, product information, and order tracking. They can automate common tasks, allowing human agents to focus on more complex and specialized customer issues.

b) Personalized Customer Interactions:

Description: AI analyses customer data and behaviour to create personalized experiences. Chatbots can recommend products, services, or content tailored to individual preferences, increasing customer engagement and satisfaction.

c) Efficient Ticket Routing:

Description: AI algorithms categorize and prioritize customer tickets based on content and sentiment analysis. This ensures that customer issues are directed to the most suitable support agents, improving response times and issue resolution.

d) 24/7 Availability:

Description: AI-driven customer service operates round the clock, providing assistance to customers in different time zones and ensuring continuous support even outside regular business hours.

e) Feedback Analysis:

Description: Sentiment analysis tools analyse customer feedback, reviews, and social media comments to gauge customer sentiment. Businesses can use this information to identify areas for improvement, track customer satisfaction, and enhance their products or services.

Challenges and Considerations:

a) Accuracy and Naturalness:

Description: Ensuring that AI responses are accurate and natural-sounding is a challenge. Overly scripted or robotic interactions can lead to customer frustration. Continuous training and fine-tuning of AI models are essential for natural language processing.

b) Data Privacy and Security:

Description: AI systems process vast amounts of customer data. Protecting customer privacy and securing sensitive information are paramount. Businesses must comply with data protection regulations and implement robust security measures.

c) Integration with Human Agents:

Description: Seamlessly integrating AI-driven customer service with human agents is crucial. Transitioning customer inquiries from bots to human agents when necessary, and ensuring a smooth handover, maintains a personalized and high-quality customer experience.

d) Cultural and Language Sensitivity:

Description: AI models must be culturally sensitive and capable of understanding various accents and dialects. Businesses operating in diverse regions need AI systems that can adapt to different languages and cultural nuances.

Future Trends in AI-Powered Customer Service:

a) Multimodal Customer Interactions:

Description: Future AI systems will support multimodal interactions, including text, voice, and visual inputs. Chatbots and virtual assistants will understand and respond to customer queries through a combination of natural language, images, and voice commands.

b) Augmented Reality (AR) and Virtual Reality (VR):

Description: AR and VR technologies combined with AI will enable immersive customer support experiences. Customers can visualize products, receive virtual assistance, and troubleshoot issues in a virtual environment, enhancing the quality of customer interactions.

c) Explainable AI in Customer Service:

Description: Explainable AI models provide clear explanations of their decisions, ensuring transparency. In customer service, this is vital for building trust. Explainable AI helps customers understand why a particular recommendation or decision was made.

d) Emotion AI:

Description: Emotion AI systems can analyse facial expressions, tone of voice, and other non-verbal cues to gauge customer emotions. AI-driven insights into customer emotions help businesses tailor responses and interactions to meet emotional needs, enhancing customer satisfaction.

AI for customer service is helping in a number of ways today, including:

- Providing 24/7 support: AI-powered chatbots and virtual assistants can provide customer support 24/7, even when human agents are not available. This is especially helpful for businesses with customers in different time zones or for businesses that need to provide support outside of regular business hours.
- Answering customer questions quickly and accurately: AI-powered chatbots and virtual assistants can answer customer questions quickly and accurately, even if the questions are complex or open-ended. This is because AI systems can be trained on large amounts of data, including customer service transcripts and knowledge bases.
- Personalizing the customer experience: AI-powered customer service tools can be used to personalize the customer experience by recommending products and services, providing targeted support, and resolving issues quickly and efficiently.
- Analysing customer feedback: AI can be used to analyse customer feedback from surveys, social media, and other sources to identify trends and areas for improvement. This information can then be used to improve the customer experience and to develop new products and services.

Here are some specific examples of how AI is being used for customer service today:

- A bank uses an AI-powered chatbot to answer customer questions about their accounts, transactions, and other banking services.
- A telecommunications company uses an AI-powered virtual assistant to help customers troubleshoot problems with their internet service, phone service, and other services.

- An e-commerce company uses an AI-powered recommendation engine to recommend products to customers based on their purchase history and browsing behaviour.
- A SaaS company uses AI to analyse customer feedback from surveys and support tickets to identify trends and areas for improvement.

Here are some specific examples of AI tools that are being used for customer service today:

- Zendesk: Zendesk offers a variety of AI-powered customer service tools, such as Zendesk Answer Bot, Zendesk Explore, and Zendesk Sunshine.
- Salesforce Service Cloud: Salesforce Service Cloud offers a variety of AI-powered customer service tools, such as Salesforce Einstein Bots, Salesforce Einstein Analytics, and Salesforce Einstein Next Best Action.
- Microsoft Dynamics 365 Customer Service: Microsoft Dynamics 365 Customer Service offers a variety of AI-powered customer service tools, such as Microsoft Power Virtual Agents, Microsoft Dynamics 365 Customer Insights, and Microsoft Dynamics 365 Customer Service Insights.

AI for customer service is a rapidly developing field, and new tools and applications are being developed all the time. As AI technology continues to improve, we can expect to see even more innovative and effective ways to use AI to improve the customer experience.

It is important to note that AI for customer service is not a replacement for human agents. AI tools can help agents to work more efficiently and effectively, but they cannot replace the human touch. However, AI can be used to free up agents to focus on more complex and strategic tasks.

Here are some AI apps names for customer service:

- Zendesk Answer Bot
- Salesforce Einstein Bots
- Microsoft Power Virtual Agents
- Amazon Lex
- Google Cloud Dialogflow
- IBM Watson Assistant
- Genesys Cloud AI
- Twilio Flex
- LivePerson Conversational AI
- Drift
- HubSpot Service Hub
- Freshdesk
- Zoho Desk

These apps use AI to provide customer service through chatbots, virtual assistants, and other channels. They can be used to answer customer questions, provide support, and resolve issues.

In addition to the above, there are many other AI-powered customer service tools that are being developed and used by businesses today. As AI technology continues to improve, we can expect to see even more innovative and effective ways to use AI for customer service.

It is important to note that AI for customer service is not a replacement for human agents. AI tools can help agents to work more efficiently and effectively, but they cannot replace the human touch. However, AI can be used to free up agents to focus on more complex and strategic tasks.

AI in customer service continues to evolve, providing businesses with powerful tools to deliver exceptional customer experiences. By leveraging AI technologies, businesses can optimize their customer support operations, increase customer satisfaction, and build lasting customer relationships.

16. Education

Artificial Intelligence (AI) has the potential to transform education by enhancing the learning experience, personalizing education, and improving educational outcomes. Here's a deeper look into the AI-powered world of education.

Components of AI in Education:

a) Intelligent Tutoring Systems:

Description: Intelligent Tutoring Systems (ITS) use AI algorithms to provide personalized tutoring to students. These systems adapt to individual learning styles, assess students' strengths and weaknesses, and offer tailored lessons and exercises to improve their understanding of the subject matter.

b) Adaptive Learning Platforms:

Description: Adaptive learning platforms use AI to analyse students' interactions and performance data. Based on this analysis, the platforms adjust the learning materials, difficulty levels, and pacing to match each student's learning needs. Adaptive learning ensures that students receive content tailored to their proficiency levels, fostering personalized learning experiences.

c) Automated Grading and Assessment:

Description: AI-powered tools automate the grading process for assignments, quizzes, and exams. Machine learning algorithms can assess written responses, code, or even creative projects, providing timely feedback to students and allowing educators to focus on teaching and providing targeted assistance.

d) Intelligent Content Creation:

Description: AI algorithms generate educational content, including textbooks, quizzes, and exercises. Natural Language Processing (NLP) and machine learning models can create interactive and engaging content, supplementing traditional educational materials.

e) Virtual Reality (VR) and Augmented Reality (AR):

Description: VR and AR technologies, combined with AI, create immersive learning experiences. AI algorithms can adapt virtual environments based on students' interactions, providing dynamic and interactive simulations for subjects like science, history, and geography.

Applications of AI in Education:

a) Personalized Learning:

Description: AI analyses students' learning behaviours, preferences, and performance data to create personalized learning paths. Personalized learning platforms adapt the curriculum, providing targeted resources and exercises to address individual strengths and weaknesses.

b) Early Intervention and Support:

Description: AI systems can identify students at risk of falling behind or struggling with specific topics. Early intervention tools provide additional resources, tutoring, or personalized exercises to help students overcome challenges and stay on track.

c) Language Processing and Translation:

Description: AI-powered language processing tools aid language learning by providing pronunciation feedback, language translation, and language practice exercises. These tools enhance language acquisition and communication skills.

d) Special Education Support:

Description: AI technologies support students with special needs by offering tailored educational materials and assistive tools. Speech recognition, text-to-speech, and customized learning interfaces cater to diverse learning requirements, ensuring inclusivity in education.

e) Teacher Professional Development:

Description: AI platforms assist teachers in professional development by analysing their teaching methods, classroom interactions, and student engagement. These insights help educators enhance their teaching strategies and create more effective learning environments.

Challenges and Considerations:

a) Data Privacy and Security:

Description: AI systems in education require access to student data. Ensuring data privacy, security, and compliance with regulations (such as FERPA in the United States) are critical considerations. Safeguarding sensitive student information is paramount.

b) Bias and Fairness:

Description: AI algorithms can inherit biases present in the training data, potentially leading to unfair treatment of students.

Addressing algorithmic biases and ensuring fairness and equity in AI-based educational tools is essential to providing equal opportunities for all learners.

c) Ethical Use of AI:

Description: Ethical considerations in AI education include transparent communication about AI use, obtaining informed consent, and ensuring that AI technologies are used to benefit students and enhance learning, rather than for purposes like surveillance or profiling.

d) Teacher-Student Balance:

Description: AI should augment, not replace, the role of teachers. Striking the right balance between technology and human interaction is crucial to maintain the mentorship and support provided by educators.

Future Trends in AI-powered Education:

a) Lifelong Learning and Upskilling:

Description: AI-powered platforms will continue to support lifelong learning and upskilling initiatives. Personalized learning paths, adaptive content, and skill assessment tools will help individuals acquire new skills and knowledge throughout their lives.

b) Collaborative Learning Environments:

Description: AI will facilitate collaborative learning by analysing students' interactions, enabling group projects, and fostering teamwork. Intelligent collaborative platforms will enhance communication and cooperation among students, promoting a sense of community in online and hybrid learning environments.

c) Emotional Intelligence AI:

Description: AI systems will be developed to recognize and respond to students' emotions. Emotionally intelligent AI can gauge students' frustration, engagement, or confusion and adapt the learning experience accordingly, offering emotional support and encouragement when needed.

d) Global Education Access:

Description: AI-powered platforms will help bridge educational disparities by providing quality education to remote and underserved communities. Online education, virtual classrooms, and AI-driven tutoring can reach students worldwide, ensuring access to educational resources and opportunities.

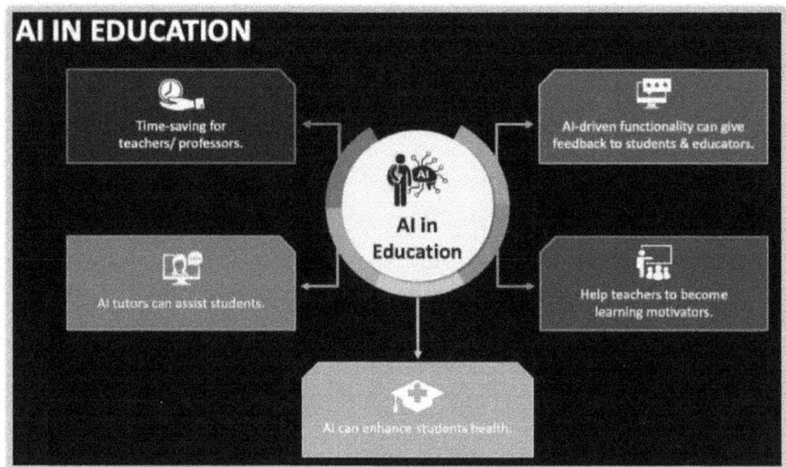

AI for education is helping in a number of ways today, including:

- Personalizing learning: AI can be used to personalize learning by adapting to each student's individual needs and learning style. For example, AI-powered tutoring systems can provide students with personalized feedback and instruction.
- Improving the quality of feedback: AI can be used to provide students with more timely and detailed feedback on their work. This can help students to improve their learning and to identify areas where they need more support.
- Automating tasks: AI can be used to automate tasks such as grading papers and providing feedback, which can free up teachers to focus on more important tasks such as lesson planning and student engagement.
- Making education more accessible: AI can be used to make education more accessible to students with disabilities and to students in remote or underserved areas. For example, AI-powered screen readers can help blind students to access educational materials.

Here are some specific examples of how AI is being used for education today:

- An AI-powered tutoring system is used to help students learn math at their own pace.
- An AI-powered writing feedback tool is used to help students improve their writing skills.
- An AI-powered translation tool is used to help students learn foreign languages.
- An AI-powered video captioning tool is used to help deaf and hard of hearing students access educational videos.

Here are some specific examples of AI tools that are being used for education today:

- DreamBox Learning: DreamBox Learning is an AI-powered adaptive learning platform that helps students learn math.
- Grammarly: Grammarly is an AI-powered writing feedback tool that helps students improve their writing skills.
- Duolingo: Duolingo is a language learning platform that uses AI to help students learn foreign languages.
- Otter.ai: Otter.ai is an AI-powered video transcription and captioning tool.

AI for education is a rapidly developing field, and new tools and applications are being developed all the time. As AI technology continues to improve, we can expect to see even more innovative and effective ways to use AI to personalize learning, improve the quality of feedback, automate tasks, and make education more accessible.

It is important to note that AI for education is not a replacement for teachers. AI tools can help teachers to be more effective, but they cannot replace the human touch.

Here are some AI apps names for education:

- DreamBox Learning
- Grammarly
- Duolingo
- Otter.ai
- Khan Academy Kids
- Osmo

- Prodigy Math Game
- ABCmouse.com
- IXL Learning
- Rosetta Stone
- Lumosity
- Memrise

These apps use AI to personalize learning, provide feedback, automate tasks, and make education more accessible. They can be used by students of all ages and abilities to learn a variety of subjects, including math, science, reading, writing, and foreign languages.

Here are some more AI apps for education, each with a specific focus:

- AI-powered tutoring systems:
    - Carnegie Learning MATHia
    - Knewton Alta
    - Knewton MathSpring
- AI-powered writing feedback tools:
    - QuillBot
    - ProWritingAid
    - PaperRater
- AI-powered translation tools:
    - Google Translate
    - Microsoft Translator
    - DeepL

- AI-powered accessibility tools:
    - Texthelp Read&Write
    - Don Johnston Snap&Read
    - Kurzweil 3000

This is just a small sample of the many AI apps that are available for education today. As AI technology continues to develop, we can expect to see even more innovative and effective ways to use AI to improve the learning experience for all students.

It is important to note that AI apps for education should be used as part of a comprehensive educational approach. AI apps can be a valuable tool for supplementing traditional teaching methods and providing students with personalized support, but they should not be used as a replacement for qualified teachers.

AI in education continues to evolve, offering innovative solutions to enhance learning experiences and empower both students and educators. As technology advances, the integration of AI will play a pivotal role in shaping the future of education, making learning more accessible, engaging, and tailored to individual needs.

In Conclusion: Embracing the Future

As we conclude our exploration into the vast landscape of the Artificial Intelligence Revolution, we find ourselves standing at the crossroads of innovation and possibility. The journey through these 16 chapters has been a captivating odyssey, unveiling the incredible strides made by AI across diverse domains. From the humble beginnings of virtual assistants to the intricate realms of predictive analytics, each chapter has been a testament to the transformative power of artificial intelligence.

In the realm of virtual assistants, we witnessed the evolution from simple task-oriented helpers to sophisticated conversational companions, capable of understanding context and intent. Recommendation systems have reshaped how we discover content, products, and experiences, enhancing our lives through personalized suggestions. The vigilant eyes of fraud detection systems tirelessly safeguard our digital transactions, showcasing the resilience of AI in the face of evolving threats.

Image and facial recognition technologies have not only revolutionized security measures but have also paved the way for innovative applications in various fields, including healthcare and law enforcement. Natural Language Processing (NLP) has granted machines the ability to comprehend and generate human-like language, fostering seamless communication between humans and machines. Machine Translation has broken down language barriers, fostering global connectivity and understanding.

The rise of voice search has transformed the way we interact with technology, making information accessible through simple spoken commands. Smart home devices have turned houses into intelligent, responsive environments, enhancing convenience and energy efficiency. Social Media Algorithms shape our online experiences, creating personalized feeds that reflect our preferences, interests, and connections.

The promise of self-driving cars continues to redefine transportation, with the potential to enhance safety, reduce traffic congestion, and revolutionize urban planning. In the field of medical diagnosis, AI has emerged as a valuable ally to healthcare professionals, providing insights and support in complex decision-making processes. Code generation and robotic process automation streamline workflows, automating routine tasks and empowering human creativity.

Predictive analytics unlocks the power of data, offering businesses valuable insights into trends, patterns, and future possibilities. AI-driven customer service has elevated the quality of interactions, providing efficient and personalized support. In the realm of education, AI opens new avenues for personalized learning experiences, catering to individual needs and preferences.

As we reflect on these advancements, it is essential to acknowledge the ethical considerations that accompany the AI revolution. Responsible development and deployment of AI technologies are paramount to ensuring that the benefits are widespread and that potential risks are mitigated. The ethical implications of bias in algorithms, data privacy concerns, and the impact on employment must be carefully navigated as we chart the course ahead.

In conclusion, the Artificial Intelligence Revolution is not just a technological phenomenon; it is a testament to human ingenuity, curiosity, and the relentless pursuit of progress. We stand on the brink of a future where AI is not just a tool but a partner, collaborator, and catalyst for positive change. The stories within these chapters are not just about machines; they are about us—our aspirations, challenges, and the boundless potential of the human-AI partnership.

As we embrace the future, let us tread with awareness, responsibility, and a commitment to harness the power of AI for the greater good. The journey does not end here; it merely transforms into the next chapter of innovation, discovery, and the continued evolution of the Artificial Intelligence Revolution.

References & Inspiration

As we delve into the intricate threads of the Artificial Intelligence Revolution, it is fitting to acknowledge the wealth of inspiration and knowledge that has woven this tapestry of technological marvels. Each chapter in this exploration has been guided by a diverse array of references, drawing from the collective wisdom of experts, pioneers, and thought leaders who have illuminated the path of AI progress.

The foundation of our journey lies in the insights provided by the luminaries and scholars who have dedicated their efforts to shaping the landscape of virtual assistants, recommendation systems, fraud detection, and beyond. From seminal research papers to groundbreaking publications, these references serve as beacons, illuminating the way forward into the uncharted territories of artificial intelligence.

In the following pages, I present a curated collection of references for each chapter, offering readers an opportunity to delve deeper into the foundations, methodologies, and breakthroughs that underpin the narrative. These references are not mere citations; they are gateways to a vast repository of knowledge that has fuelled the evolution of AI across industries and disciplines.

As we pay homage to the thinkers and innovators who have paved the way, let these references be a testament to the collaborative spirit of the AI community—a global symphony of minds harmonizing to orchestrate the future of technology.

Chapter-wise references

Chapter-1: Virtual Assistants

- *Chat GPT -* *https://chat.openai.com/*
- *Google Bard-* *https://bard.google.com/*
- Image from –

  https://www.nitcoinc.com/blog/key-technologies-to-drive-artificial-intelligence-virtual-assistants/

Chapter-2: Recommendation Systems

- *Chat GPT -* *https://chat.openai.com/*
- *Google Bard-* *https://bard.google.com/*
- Image from –

  https://becominghuman.ai/how-ai-based-recommendation-engine-helps-transform-user-experience-928f9761d4b7

Chapter-3: Fraud detection

- *Chat GPT -* *https://chat.openai.com/*
- *Google Bard-* *https://bard.google.com/*
- Image from –

https://www.pentasecurity.com/blog/fraud-detection-system-fds-with-ai-technology/

Chapter-4: Image and facial recognition

- *Chat GPT -* *https://chat.openai.com/*
- *Google Bard-* *https://bard.google.com/*
- Image from –

  https://www.linkedin.com/pulse/facial-recognition-ai-use-your-expressions-judge-glen-gilmore/

Chapter-5: Natural language processing (NLP)

- *Chat GPT -* *https://chat.openai.com/*
- *Google Bard-* *https://bard.google.com/*
- Image from –

  https://www.xoriant.com/blog/natural-language-processing-the-next-disruptive-technology-under-ai-part-i

Chapter-6: Machine Translation

- *Chat GPT -* *https://chat.openai.com/*
- *Google Bard-* *https://bard.google.com/*
- Image from –

  https://crowdin.com/blog/2023/06/29/ai-translation-assistant

- https://www.google.com/search?q=AI+apps+for+machine+translation#ip=1

Chapter-7: Voice search

- *Chat GPT* - *https://chat.openai.com/*
- *Google Bard*- *https://bard.google.com/*
- Image from –

  https://www.yourdigitalresource.com/post/ai-for-voice-search-optimization

Chapter-8: Smart home devices

- *Chat GPT* - *https://chat.openai.com/*
- *Google Bard*- *https://bard.google.com/*
- Image from –

  https://www.analyticsinsight.net/how-artificial-intelligence-is-enabling-smart-homes/

Chapter-9: Social Media Algorithms

- *Chat GPT* - *https://chat.openai.com/*
- *Google Bard*- *https://bard.google.com/*
- Image from –

https://www.consagous.co/blog/how-ai-ml-are-transforming-social-media

Chapter-10: Self-driving cars

- *Chat GPT* - *https://chat.openai.com/*

- *Google Bard- https://bard.google.com/*
- Image from –

  https://bernardmarr.com/how-tesla-is-using-artificial-intelligence-to-create-the-autonomous-cars-of-the-future/

Chapter-11: Medical diagnosis

- *Chat GPT - https://chat.openai.com/*
- *Google Bard- https://bard.google.com/*
- Image from –

  https://www.linkedin.com/pulse/ai-powered-medical-diagnosis-dataemr-management-using-sreenivasan/

Chapter-12: Code generation

- *Chat GPT - https://chat.openai.com/*
- *Google Bard- https://bard.google.com/*
- Image from –

https://aws.amazon.com/blogs/machine-learning/reinventing-the-data-experience-use-generative-ai-and-modern-data-architecture-to-unlock-insights/

Chapter-13: Robotic process automation

- *Chat GPT - https://chat.openai.com/*
- *Google Bard- https://bard.google.com/*
- Image from –

https://www.epsoftinc.com/combining-artificial-intelligence-and-robotic-process-automation-rpa/

Chapter-14: Predictive analytics

- *Chat GPT* - *https://chat.openai.com/*
- *Google Bard*- *https://bard.google.com/*
- Image from –

https://www.process.st/what-is-predictive-analytics/

Chapter-15: Customer service

- *Chat GPT* - *https://chat.openai.com/*
- *Google Bard*- *https://bard.google.com/*
- Image from –

https://maxicus.com/importance-of-artificial-intelligence-in-customer-service/

Chapter-16: Education

- *Chat GPT* - *https://chat.openai.com/*
- *Google Bard*- *https://bard.google.com/*
- Image from –

https://www.collidu.com/presentation-ai-in-education

A Request to The Reader

May I ask you for a small favour?

I would like to thank you from the bottom of my heart for having bought and read my book. I hope this book has met your expectations and given you a good insight and knowledge regarding Artificial Intelligence, its adaption, and a few examples along with how to leverage this platform to thrive your day-to-day life or carrier.

I request you to provide me your valuable rating and a review of the book on the amazon / Flipkart site or wherever you purchased. Your feedback would inspire and encourage me in my author-journey, where I will look forward to enhancing your knowledge, skills and positively impact lives of many professionals.

Thank you once again. Wish you all success and happiness in your life.

About the Author

Subhranshu Pati, the accomplished author of "Artificial Intelligence Revolution," is a seasoned professional with a remarkable career spanning 17 years. A dynamic force in the realm of Information Technology, Subhranshu has excelled as a Business Analyst, demonstrating a keen understanding of the intricacies of the Shipping and Logistics domain.

Throughout his illustrious journey, Subhranshu has not only amassed extensive experience but has also been at the forefront of global leadership. As a leader of the application and support team, he has steered initiatives on a global scale, playing a pivotal role in shaping and optimizing technology solutions for the challenges inherent to the Shipping and Logistics sector.

In his book, "Artificial Intelligence Revolution," Subhranshu leverages his wealth of practical experience to provide readers with profound insights into the transformative power of AI. With a focus on real-world applications, he explores the intersection of technology and logistics, offering a unique perspective on the evolution of Artificial Intelligence in the industry.

Subhranshu's expertise extends beyond the technical realm; his leadership and strategic vision have been instrumental in driving innovation and efficiency within the global Information Technology landscape. His commitment to excellence is evident not only in his professional achievements but also in his dedication to sharing knowledge and shaping the discourse on the future of technology.

"Artificial Intelligence Revolution" is a testament to Subhranshu Pati's ability to bridge the gap between theory and practice, making complex technological concepts accessible to a diverse audience. Through this book, he invites readers to join him on a journey into the boundless possibilities that AI presents for the future.

www.ingramcontent.com/pod-product-compliance
Lightning Source LLC
LaVergne TN
LVHW021154160826
845679LV00024B/2114

* 9 7 9 8 8 9 2 3 3 6 9 4 9 *